LifeCaps Presents:

Turing

The Tragic Life of Alan Turing

By Fergus Mason

BookCaps™ Study Guides

www.bookcaps.com

FERGUS MASON

Turing

Table of Contents

ABOUT LIFECAPS

LifeCaps is an imprint of BookCaps™ Study Guides. With each book, a lesser known or sometimes forgotten life is recapped. We publish a wide array of topics (from baseball and music to literature and philosophy), so check our growing catalogue regularly (www.bookcaps.com) to see our newest books.

CHAPTER 1: SECRET WHISPERS

The Roman lawyer and statesman Marcus Cicero once said "*Nervos belli, pecuniam infinitam*" – "The sinews of war, unlimited money." That was as true then as it is now. Waging war is an incredibly expensive business. In 1941, the sinews of the British Empire were creaking under the strain; standing almost alone against Nazi Germany and its inexorable expansion across Europe, Britain was near bankruptcy, kept afloat only by draconian rationing and a steady flow of aid from the USA.

If war is thought of as a body it needs more than sinews, though. It needs a nervous system as well, to transmit commands from the brain – the commanders – to the armored fists that will carry them out. It's also vital that the enemy can't read those commands or he'll know what to expect, a vital edge that can change the course of the war. The most brilliant plan is useless if the enemy know it ahead of time. The nerves of war are secure communications, and with its troops scattered from the

Spanish border to the gates of Moscow – a distance of nearly 2,000 miles – and submarines operating right up to the US coast, the Nazis faced a huge challenge in communicating secretly.

It was a challenge that, with typical German innovation and efficiency, they had worked very hard to meet. In every major headquarters across their growing empire, in the operations room of every air base, on board every warship and U-Boat, sat a varnished wooden box. Inside was a complex electromechanical device that could turn plain text into a gibberish stream of random-seeming letters, or restore sense from an incoming coded message. This was the Enigma machine. In total, Germany manufactured over 40,000 of them and throughout the war they generated tens of millions of messages, each one encyphered by a fiendishly complex transmutation that changed every day.

Cypher machines were nothing new. Substitution tables went back thousands of years, and Thomas Jefferson developed an early mechanical device – the Jefferson Wheel – that was in use with the US Army until 1945. What made the Enigma different was the incredible complexity of its mechanism, and the number of separate transformations it imposed on the text. Even the simplest military machine changed each letter nine times on its way through the circuits, and at every key press the machine reconfigured itself so the next letter would be encoded with a completely different cypher. Even if a machine fell into British hands it would be useless without the key settings, which changed every day. To read an intercepted message, the British would have to know how the machine had been set up, and if the wrong setting was chosen it would simply spit out more gibberish. Guessing the settings was hopeless – there were 1,074,584,913,000,000,000,000,000 possible start configurations and only one of them would work. It's hardly surprising that the Germans believed, right to the end, that Enigma was unbreakable.

But they were wrong. Unknown to them it had first been cracked as early as 1932, although that was an older, simpler model. A brilliant team at the Polish Cypher Bureau had found a tiny weakness in the system and managed to exploit it. It was hard, painstaking work and success was never guaranteed, but with luck, Enigma could be broken. Of course, by the time war broke out in 1939, the machines themselves, and the operating procedures for them, had been improved. The volume of messages had also expanded massively, and the Polish techniques – even with the aid of the machines they'd built to automate the process – were just too slow to handle the traffic.

But, unknown to the Nazis – and to almost anyone else until the 1970s – the British had their own techniques. By 1941, they'd made a series of significant breakthroughs that ripped the Enigma cypher wide open, and were now decoding messages on an industrial scale. These breakthroughs weren't the result of a commando raid or espionage operation to steal Enigma's secrets; they were the work of a group of university professors, telephone engineers and crossword fanatics. The driving force behind this odd group was one man – a mild-mannered, eccentric mathematician from the University of Cambridge. This man, an undeniable genius whose later life was plagued by controversy and tragedy, probably played a greater role in the eventual Allied victory than anyone else. Until quite recently, his contribution to the war effort was barely recognized. Everyone's heard of Churchill, Eisenhower, Montgomery, Patton and even de Gaulle, but far fewer have ever heard of Alan Turing.

CHAPTER 2: SCHOOL DAYS

In the early 20th century, the British Empire was at the height of its size and power. A quarter of the world's land surface was either British dominions or colonies directly ruled from London. The Union flag flew from Canada to Cape Town, from the Falkland Islands in the South Atlantic to Hong Kong on the Chinese coast. The jewel in the crown was India, a massive land with a huge population and plentiful resources. It was self-governing but under the ultimate authority of the British government, and its civil service was a mixture of Indian and British administrators. Firm ties formed between the natives and the colonists, who each began to adopt the other's culture to some extent – the British love of curry and the upper-class tradition of playing polo both date from this time, and the modern state of India's military and civil service are both built firmly on the British model – but each also preserved their own identity. For many of the Britons who built their careers in the distant provinces of the Raj, a major part of that identity was the value of being born in the mother country. So it was that when Ethel Turing was expecting her second son in 1912, her husband Julius took leave from his Indian Civil Service job in Chatrapur, and the couple made the long sea voyage back to England. It gave them a chance to spend some time with their older son, John, who was living with a retired British Army officer and his wife in Hastings. The family rented a house in the London district of Maida Vale and prepared for the birth.

Today, 2 Warrington Crescent is the Colonnade Hotel, an upscale boutique hotel in a part of Maida Vale known as Little Venice for the houseboats on a nearby canal. The Colonnade has attracted its share of famous guests over the years, including John F. Kennedy,[i] psychiatrist Sigmund Freud, and any number of actors and musicians. It's a handsome Victorian building of brick and Portland stone, painted in a light cream color and embellished with neoclassical pillars and cornices, and looks like the archetype of a London luxury hotel. In fact, it started life as two large town houses in 1865, was briefly used as a boarding school then became the Warrington Lodge Medical and Surgery Home for Ladies.[ii] It finally became a hotel in 1935.

On June 23, 1912, Ethel Turing went into labor and her husband called a taxi to take her to the Warrington Lodge. A healthy son was born later that day; Ethel and Julius named him Alan Mathison Turing.

Julius had taken extended leave to come to London with his wife, but he still held a post in Chatrapur, and eventually he had to return there. After long discussions over how to handle matters, the elder Turings decided that Julius should return to India but leave his family in England, and return to visit them whenever he could. They felt that would give their sons a more "normal" education than returning to India as a family. Chitrapur was the colonial headquarters of Bihar and Orissa Province, a remote area in northeast India that now sits on the border with Bangladesh; unlike in a major city there were few Europeans there and the Turing boys would have had few other children to socialize with. In England they could go to school and make friends.

Ethel settled in Hastings with the boys and set about bringing them up. It wasn't long before she started to notice personality characteristics in Alan that marked him as different from his brother. He was incredibly inquisitive at a very young age, although this was often mistaken for mischief. He made connections between things and tried out new ideas. Having seen his mother plant seeds he tried "planting" broken toys in the hope of growing a replacement, although Ethel probably saw that as him trying to hide the evidence.[iii] He also mastered more conventional skills at incredible speed; he taught himself to read in only three weeks. He developed a very early and intense interest in numbers, and loved the way they could be ordered into sequences. When he discovered that all the street lamps in Hastings had a serial number stamped on their iron pillars, the result was disruption every time the family went for a walk, as Alan insisted on stopping to check the number on each lamp they passed. Already, as a preschooler, he was thinking about how numbers fitted together. It was an interest that would last his entire life.

When Alan was six his parents enrolled him at St. Michael's, a private elementary school in the St. Leonard's area of Hastings. St. Michael's School closed long ago but the building that housed it, a large Victorian townhouse, still stands at 20 Charles Road. As large as the building is for a residence it's not very big for a school, but that was typical of private elementaries at the time. The small size also allowed teachers to pay more attention to individual students, and it was soon obvious to the headmistress that Turing was an extremely intelligent boy. Ethel had chosen St. Michael's because she wanted Alan to learn Latin, but while he did well in all subjects, his special aptitude was for mathematics.

Schools – or good ones, at least – teach a lot more than just knowledge and critical thinking. They also socialize their students, and in his time at St. Michael's, many elements of Turing's character began to develop. Although highly intelligent, he was also shy, something he never managed to get over. He quickly developed a dedication to the idea of fairness though, and from an early age he saw rules as a tool to achieve this. He also seems to have found rules comforting, and quickly became indignant when they were violated – even if they were unspoken ones, or structures he had developed himself. Once, when he was still a small child, Ethel was reading to him from John Bunyan's *The Pilgrim's Progress*. It's remarkable enough that she would read something so complex and nuanced to a young boy, because the complexities and layered meanings of the book are enough to defeat many adults. At one point, she decided to leave out some of the more tortuous theology, thinking it would be too much for him, but Alan immediately objected. Skipping parts was against the "rules" of reading, he thought, and ruined the story.

When he was ten, Alan moved on to Hazelhurst School, a preparatory school just outside the village of Frant, twenty miles north of Hastings. Hazelhurst was a boarding school, and with both her sons now there, Ethel began spending more time in India with Julius. Alan kept them amused with a constant stream of quirky letters, in which he described ideas he'd had for improving devices like fountain pens and typewriters. His father wrote back encouragingly, suggesting new experiments for him to try. On one occasion, following one of his father's hints, he borrowed some surveying equipment and worked out a way to measure the height of the trees in the school grounds with it.[iv] Unlike many mathematicians, whose thoughts exist in an abstract world of pure numbers, Turing was capable of bridging the gap back to the real world and using his abilities to solve real problems. Of course, any engineer does that every day, but it's unusual in a mathematician of the level that Turing would reach.

He wasn't going to reach that level at Hazelhurst, though. The goals of the school were solidly classical, aimed at turning out well-rounded members of society who could write a grammatically correct letter, correctly decline Latin verbs, and walk away from a sports match, winner or loser, with the correct attitude. Science and mathematics didn't feature strongly in the curriculum. The boys learned basic calculus, and went for nature rambles in the leafy countryside surrounding the school, but for someone with Turing's abilities there was nothing to challenge him and spur his development. He did well at sports, though, even if he was easily distracted; a sketch made by Ethel in spring 1923 shows him, field hockey stick in hand, peering curiously at a daisy on the pitch while his teammates fight for the ball behind him.

At thirteen, Turing moved on from preparatory school. His next destination was Sherborne, an ancient public school[1] in the small Dorset town of the same name. Founded in the early 8th century by Saint Aldhelm, Sherborne claims King Alfred the Great among its former pupils. Today, the school's buildings include the remains of a Benedictine monastery it was associated with from the 10th to 16th centuries. Like Hazelhurst, Sherborne was a traditional boarding school that focused heavily on a classical education and on preparing boys to go on to university, with an expectation that they would qualify for Oxford or Cambridge. It was a very prestigious school, and Turing was excited at the thought of going there. It wouldn't be an easy journey, though.

In the first half of the 20th century, Britain was one of the world's leading producers and exporters of coal. Production began to fall in the 1920s, as other nations increased their own exports and supplied markets that had been buying from Britain. Falling profits translated into falling wages for miners, and the powerful mineworkers' union pressured the Trades Union Congress into demanding government subsidies for their pay packets. A one-month temporary subsidy was agreed but

---

[1] In England a public school is an elite fee-paying school. The UK equivalent of a US public school is called a state school.

the miners and the TUC demanded it be made permanent. Unfortunately for them, the government had used the month to prepare, and felt it was in a strong enough position to refuse the union demands. On May 3, 1926 Britain's only general strike began. It collapsed in only ten days as volunteers took over essential services, but from May 3 to May 13 there were serious disruptions to heavy manufacturing and transport.

That was bad news for Turing, because the new term at Sherborne started on May 3 and the family was now living in Southampton, 60 miles away. The transport workers had come out in sympathy with the miners, and there were no buses or trains. Ethel couldn't drive, so it looked as if Alan wouldn't be able to get to school until the strike ended or the railway and bus companies found replacement drivers. That was underestimating his determination though. He was a strong cyclist, so he decided to make the trip on his bike. He was loaded down with a rucksack full of clothes and books, and had to navigate his way along miles of country roads; it wasn't an easy journey. He made it, though. Setting out on Sunday, May 2, it took him two days. He spent the night in a hotel near Shaftesbury and continued on his way next morning. When Sherborne's new students lined up to register late on the Monday afternoon, Alan Turing was among them.

Unfortunately, his time at Sherborne wasn't, academically, all it could have been. He struggled at the subjects the school focused on; in his third year he came bottom in English and second from bottom in Latin. Even in math and science he annoyed his teachers, by ignoring the tasks they set and investigating things he found more interesting. In fact, he was progressing at a rate his teachers probably couldn't comprehend. Still shy, he spent little time socializing with the other boys in his year. Instead, he was constantly in the library, reading voraciously. On one of his informal study sessions, two years after arriving at Sherborne, he picked up a book that by rights shouldn't have been in a school library at all. Published in German in 1916 by a young professor at the Berlin Academy of Sciences, the advanced concepts in physics it described were far beyond the majority of scientists at the time, and certainly should have been out of reach of a teenager. The book was an English translation of Albert Einstein's *Relativität*.

In 1928, physics was still dominated by classical mechanics, the laws of motion described in the 17th century by Sir Isaac Newton. When Einstein published *Relativity* he was very careful to avoid any mention of these laws; the book wasn't an academic publication meant to be consulted by professors and researchers, but a popular science book aimed at a larger audience. It was roughly equivalent to Stephen Hawking's 1988 *A Brief History of Time*, a book that tried to explain challenging concepts in ordinary language, and Einstein hoped it would build a wider understanding of his work. He certainly didn't want it to be too controversial, so he left out some of his opinions about Newtonian physics.

He didn't leave out enough to fool Turing. Reading the book – and understanding it! – the teenager picked up the message that Einstein was leaving unstated: the German physicist believed that Newton had been wrong. Einstein seems to have counted on the fact that everyone accepted Newton's laws without question to gloss over this fact, but with his natural curiosity Turing didn't accept *anything* without question; he realized that many of Einstein's experiments and equations were designed to test Newton's laws. Why test them? The nature of the tests, to Turing, suggested only one possibility: Einstein doubted the basic principles that had supported physics for over 300 years. His deduction was absolutely correct.[v]

Turing could pick up on Einstein's doubts because he had a truly open mind; he wasn't credulous, but he was willing to challenge and reconsider even things he firmly believed. He rejected the idea that something must be true simply because of who said it. Newton's laws had been accepted for centuries, and were accurate enough for most purposes (and still are – when NASA sent Apollo 11 to the moon in 1969 they used Newtonian physics to calculate the mission, because the extra work required to use relativistic physics wasn't worth the effort) but if new research showed they were wrong, why, they were wrong. Even Einstein himself wasn't immune to Turing's iconoclastic tendencies; he reformulated one of the equations he found in the book to make it easier to understand. He also worked out Einstein's geodesic equation of motion, which wasn't in the book – it replaces Newton's First Law of motion.

The same year he discovered Einstein's work, Turing moved up into Sherborne's Sixth Form. This two-year period is traditionally when English students study for and sit the exams that decide if they can go to university or not. In 1928 that was the Higher School Certificate. While the School Certificates that students sat in the Fifth Form were fairly generalist qualifications, in Sixth Form they were allowed to specialize more, and Turing weighted his courses toward his favorite areas of science and mathematics. That was to lead this brilliant but shy boy towards one of the defining relationships in his life.

Christopher Morcom was one year in front, but with Turing in the Sixth they were now in some of the same classes. Turing had seen Morcom around the school and been struck by his appearance, a hint of same-sex attraction he later identified as the first sign that he was gay. Morcom was small for his age, lightly built in contrast to the muscular, athletic Turing, and he was plagued with illness. Turing had noticed that in 1927, he had been away from school for a while and returned looking thin and drawn. However, Morcom was a confident, lively boy and the shy Turing had never dared start a conversation with him. Now, realizing they had a shared passion for mathematics and science, he managed to overcome his reserve and approach him. With a common interest they could discuss for hours, the two quickly started to bond.

In 1929, Turing advanced to the Upper Sixth, the final run-up to the dreaded Higher Certificate exams. Because of his frequent illness, Morcom was also still in the Upper Sixth, and now they were in the same class for several subjects. Turing began working things so he could sit beside his friend and they kept each other busy by setting problems to solve, often far in advance of what the school was giving them. Pages from Turing's old school notebooks show that when they were supposed to be learning French they were, instead, discussing advanced concepts in Euclidian geometry and playing tic-tac-toe.

For Turing, his friendship with Morcom was a revelation. All his life he had been shy and withdrawn, but suddenly he had someone he could share his thoughts with. There's no doubt he was physically attracted to the older boy but he also reveled in the meeting of minds. Here was someone who wouldn't be intimidated – or, worse, bored – when Turing discussed Pi, which he'd calculated to 36 decimal places. Here was someone who shared both his enthusiasm for, and understanding of, Einstein's theories. Morcom also taught him intellectual discipline. Turing had boundless enthusiasm for the subjects that interested him, but his work was often careless. Morcom took a much more rigorous approach, which he carefully passed on. Turing, keen to impress, worked hard to learn these vital lessons. By all accounts he succeeded. His school work suddenly began to improve out of all recognition, astonishing his teachers with a new methodical approach to problem solving. His grades in math and science had always been let down by sloppy errors and cut corners but now he became more focused. His intellect and energy were now being fine-tuned into something genuinely formidable.

In December 1929, Turing and Morcom travelled to Cambridge together for a week. While most universities admitted students based on their Higher Certificate results, for the elite colleges of Oxbridge this was just the first hurdle. Applicants who had a satisfactory school grade then had to sit the universities' own entrance exams, as well as survive an often grueling interview. The two teenagers both hoped to get through the process and be accepted to study mathematics. In fact, Turing wrote that he was as excited by the thought of spending a week with Morcom as about going to Cambridge.[vi]

Nevertheless, he was geared up for the exam and interview. First, though, the two stopped off in London. They visited Morcom's mother at her sculpture studio, and "helped" her with a marble bust. Then they caught the train to Cambridge.

The trip turned out to have mixed results. Morcom was offered a scholarship and a place at Trinity College, but Turing didn't quite make it through. That was a blow, but not a fatal one; public schools offered an extra year for students to prepare for the exams, so he could sit it again in 1930. He might get to Cambridge a year behind Morcom, but he would get there and they could continue their friendship and shared enjoyment of science.

He didn't know that tragedy was just round the corner.

Before the development of antibiotics, tuberculosis was one of the most feared diseases in advanced countries. Improvements in hygiene had eliminated plagues like cholera from British towns, but every cough or sneeze might carry the deadly curse of *Mycobacterium tuberculosis*. Once infected, there was no cure; all that could be done was to protect the scarred lungs from pollution. Even then, many people wasted away and died. Others succumbed suddenly, as the infection weakened the pulmonary artery until it finally burst and caused massive, irreversible internal bleeding. Sadly, children were often the most at risk; in addition to the familiar human forms of the disease, spread by tiny droplets in exhaled air, there was a bovine form – and up to 40 per cent of Britain's dairy cattle were infected. The bacteria sometimes found their way into the milk; until pasteurization became common, one drink could transmit it. Chris

Morcom's absences from school were caused by a case of bovine TB he'd picked up a few years earlier, and on February 7, 1930, only weeks after the trip to Cambridge, he suddenly became extremely ill. Turing believed he had seen a premonition of Morcom's death in a setting moon early that morning, and within a week that fear came true; Morcom died on February 13.[vii]

Turing was devastated. After lonely years at school he'd finally found companionship, and suddenly it had been snatched away from him. It was an enormous blow and it shattered many of his dearest beliefs. Until this point he had been conventionally religious, a typical low-key Church of England worshipper. Now he found that he could no longer accept the idea of a supreme being who would allow such a senseless death. His faith was wiped away by his grief and anger. For the rest of his life he was a convinced atheist, but at the same time he never quite gave up the idea of mind and body as being separate. Three days after Morcom's death, he wrote to his mother that he was sure he would meet him again sometime, and in 1932 he repeated the same belief in a long letter to Morcom's family. His beliefs about the survival of the spirit were a long, long way from those of Christianity, though, and they were to have a profound influence on his later work. "Personally I think that spirit is really eternally connected with matter," he wrote, "but certainly not always by the same kind of body." Years afterwards it would raise a new and fascinating question: could spirit reside in a machine?

As crushed as he was by Morcom's death, Turing gradually recovered and in December 1930 he traveled up to Cambridge once more. This time he handled the interview more competently and was offered a place at the university's King's College. He had a few more months at Sherborne and a long summer vacation, and then in October 1931, he packed his belongings again and set off for Cambridge one more time.

CHAPTER 3: CAMBRIDGE

Turing had found school difficult in many ways: the constant bustle of being surrounded by hundreds of other boys, the tightly managed study, and the constrained expectations of what students should be learning. His innate intelligence, plus Morcom's guidance, had managed to carry him through, but it had been a struggle for him. He must have also been suffering internal conflicts as the fact he was gay slowly dawned on him – an immense stigma in the more socially conservative atmosphere of the time.

Now he found himself in a completely different environment. Like the schools he had attended, King's wasn't coeducational; the first female students weren't admitted there until 1972. In 1931 it was a thoroughly masculine place, with a strong tradition of sports and an atmosphere of pure academic inquiry that suited Turing perfectly. It was also a fairly closed society; the college was a self-governing world of its own within the larger world of the University of Cambridge, and its inhabitants were insulated to a large degree from the nation around them. Eccentricities, shyness and unconventional lifestyles were all tolerated and, best of all, the tutors expected students to specialize. Nobody at King's College was going to criticize Turing for ignoring French verbs; if he wanted to concentrate exclusively on ever more advanced mathematics, that was just fine.

A modern university is a huge institution, often with thousands of students scattered across large campuses. They attend lectures in huge halls, eat in a cafeteria or local fast food joints, live at home or in student residences. Cambridge in the 1930s was very different. With only a few hundred undergraduates – today there are 420 – the college was a much calmer, more intimate place. Students lived in large private rooms inside the college buildings and ate together in a grand dining hall. Lectures might have only a dozen attendees, and much more work was done individually or in one-on-one tutoring sessions. Degrees were more loosely structured, with students – even at the bachelor degree level – able to follow their own interests to a much greater extent than they can today. Undergraduates, grad students and academics socialized together in a professor's private study or in the college's two bars. The porters, often retired Army NCOs, made sure their young charges got their mail and were kept supplied with beer and sherry; a large domestic staff looked after their housekeeping. The microsociety of the college was also a very tolerant one, largely free of the conservatism of the wider British public. If a student was attracted to other men, well, that's the way he was. Nobody at King's, either other students or the faculty, was going to get very excited about it. With this sudden freedom, it was at King's College that Turing really came into his own.

By 1932 Turing had moved even further forward in science and mathematics. Now with a solid grounding in relativity – which accurately describes the behavior of large objects – he had recently discovered quantum mechanics through the work of John Von Neumann, a field of science that began by looking at the behavior of light and now explains the behavior of matter at the subatomic level. Modern electronics, including microprocessors, work on quantum principles. That's not unrelated to the fact that Turing wondered if quantum mechanics, and the idea that particles and waves are essentially the same thing, formed the bridge between mind and matter. In 1933, he started working through *Principia Mathematica* by Bertrand Russell and Alfred North Whitehead, a key work on the logical basis of mathematics.

Russell, a former Cambridge lecturer, was a controversial figure. He'd been dismissed from Trinity College for holding pacifist views during the First World War, travelled to the newly-born Soviet Union as an interested socialist, and been in trouble in the USA (where he worked between the wars as a professor in Chicago and Los Angeles) for "sexual immorality". He was still influential at Cambridge, though. The Oxbridge universities had a reputation for anti-establishment thought between the wars, and in fact, some of Britain's most famous traitors – Philby, Blunt, Burgess and Maclean – were recruited there by the Soviets in the early 1930s, while Turing was an undergraduate. Blunt and Burgess were both gay, while Maclean was bisexual, and there was some overlap between the circle of openly gay students and the leftist political groups. Turing himself flirted with the anti-war movement, which was supported by Russell and many other academics, but drew back from any involvement in Marxism; his politics as an undergraduate were center-left, but he wasn't a communist and didn't have any sympathies with the USSR. He was also completely dedicated to mathematics, so the shadowy recruiters from the NKVD would probably have overlooked him – the Soviet Union had excellent mathematicians of its own – and the intelligence agency was more interested in those who planned to join the British government.

Even if Turing had been of interest to the Soviets it's unlikely he would have been drawn into their web. In addition to his less radical politics, he also mostly stayed away from the gay scene. While he fully came to terms with his homosexuality at Cambridge, and had a sporadic affair with fellow mathematician James Atkins, he didn't really fit into that group. Most of the gay undergraduates spent their time in literary discussion groups and other intellectual hobbies, and that really wasn't Turing's style; he was much more of an athlete. By now he was tall, powerfully built and in outstanding physical shape, and he enthusiastically joined in the college's sporting activities. In addition to running he took up the classic Oxbridge sport, rowing, and later learned to sail a dinghy too. While his lover Atkins discussed Tolstoy over sherry in someone's study, Turing was much more likely to be out on the rippling waters of the River Cam, legs and back straining as he helped propel one of the fast, light eight-oar boats.

At the same time, he was putting just as much effort into his degree. In late 1933 and early 1934, with his final exams approaching, he started pulling everything he'd learned together into a solid understanding of his highly specialized subject. The work paid off. In summer 1934 he graduated with a first-class honors degree in mathematics. Now he had to decide what to do next.

In the end he chose the simplest option: he just stayed at Cambridge. For another year he lived in King's College, carrying on with his research, and writing a dissertation that, he hoped, would earn him a permanent place at the university. Now he was concentrating on the central limit theorem, part of probability theory. The theorem states that if a sufficiently large number of random numbers are collected and analyzed they will form a "normal distribution" – what's usually known as a bell curve. Turing's aim was to prove that the theorem was true. Unknown to him it had already been proven, twelve years earlier, by the Finnish mathematician Jarl Waldemar Lindeberg. That should have made Turing's work worthless, because a dissertation as expected to be a piece of original research. He was lucky, though. When he presented his paper to the college, they were impressed enough with his approach to the problem that they accepted it. As a result, in 1935 Turing was elected as a Fellow of King's College.

In most universities, a fellow is a researcher or junior teaching faculty, but at Oxbridge they're members of their college's governing body. They also have some privileges that make the position very valuable to anyone who wants to follow an academic career. Two of the most significant are the right to eat at the high table in the college's dining hall, together with the staff, and free accommodation. With a suite of rooms – bedroom, bathroom and study – and guaranteed meals, Turing now had a secure position to pursue his research. In exchange for a small income, he was expected to help with tutoring students, but the rest of his time was his own. He found plenty to fill it with.

Most people find it hard to get too excited about math, but sometimes it can have profound implications. One of the most interesting early 20th century mathematicians was David Hilbert, a professor at Göttingen in Germany. One of his specialty subjects was infinity, which he explained with a system that's now known as Hilbert's Hotel. In this slightly quirky model the implications of limitless numbers are explained in the context of a hotel which has an infinite number of rooms – and when you arrive they're all full. Hilbert's genius was in taking concepts that can't even be explained in a way that makes any sense, and turning them into real-world problems that people can relate to. For example, if you arrive at Hilbert's Hotel on your own, the manager can find you a room easily; all he does is ask all the existing guests to move up one room number. The person in Room 1 moves into Room 2, the person in Room 2 moves into Room 3 and so on; the person in Room 1,274,974,230,643,021 moves into 1,274,974,230,643,022. That leaves Room 1 available for you. Hilbert went on to explain how to find rooms for any number of people arriving (if there are n guests, move the existing guests up n numbers) and even an infinite number of new guests. He didn't exactly make advanced math fun, but he certainly made it comprehensible. Turing loved his approach, and was also intrigued by some of the challenges he set for his peers. One of these, devised by Hilbert in 1928, went by the forbidding German name of *Entscheidungsproblem.*

The *Entscheidungsproblem* – the Decision Problem – is a fiendish blend of mathematics and logic. To solve it would require an algorithm capable of deciding whether or not a mathematical statement is universally valid. Its usefulness in ordinary life is exactly zero, but Hilbert just liked setting challenges and Turing, now quietly established as one of Britain's leading mathematicians, liked solving them. He spent nearly a year on the *Entscheidungsproblem* before he reached his conclusion; it couldn't be solved. In April 1936 he presented his paper to Professor M.H.A. Newman, who had pointed him toward the problem in the first place, and for the second time in his short career was told that he'd been beaten to his conclusion. Newman had just received a paper from the American mathematician Alonzo Church, which also concluded that the problem could not be solved. Turing had to add a reference to Church's work to his own paper, and its publication was delayed until August, leaving Church the clear winner of the competition to solve Hilbert's puzzle. The solution to the *Entscheidungsproblem* is now known as the Church-Turing thesis. In fact, though, the young Englishman's paper was far more significant. Church had solved the problem using standard assumptions in theoretical mathematics; his solution was purely paper-based. Turing had started off by restating and simplifying an attempt at the problem by another German, Kurt Gödel, but had then changed direction. He started thinking about ways to solve the *Entscheidungsproblem* by using a device that could, theoretically at least, actually be built. He called these devices, which he imagined would be fed information using a punched paper tape, A-Machines (the A is for *Automatic*). Modern mathematicians give credit where it's due; they call hypothetical versions, still used in many research problems, Turing Machines. As for those that aren't hypothetical, and have actually been built, they have a different name. We call them computers.

CHAPTER 4: PRINCETON

Turing, perhaps influenced by his views on matter and spirit, was strongly drawn to the idea of machines that could process information. Calculating machines – and even primitive computers - already existed, of course; Charles Babbage had produced plans for his programmable Difference Engine in 1822, and the Royal Navy's battleships had been fitted with electromechanical fire control computers since before the First World War. The concept of the Turing Machine was different. Turing also called it the Universal Machine, because his vision was for a device that, with the right programming, would compute anything that *could* be computed. As a hypothetical device, it was a useful aid to mathematicians. Turing wasn't satisfied with hypotheticals. He wanted to turn his vision into reality. The best way to do that, he decided, was to go to the USA.

There's a long history of exchanges between US and British universities. With a shared language, and academic cultures that are similar enough to be compatible but different enough to inject each other with fresh, often revolutionary ideas, it's natural for both students and professors to cross the Atlantic for a few years. In September 1936, Turing traveled to Princeton University to study under Alonzo Church.

It was a productive partnership. Church had already been teaching at Princeton for nine years and had a massive in-depth knowledge of computational theory. Turing was younger and less experienced but had a gift for making new insights and deductive leaps. Their personal relationship seems to have been an uneasy one. Church described Turing as a "rather odd" loner, and the Englishman was certainly shy, but he seemed to have a lively enough social life around the graduate school.[viii] It just didn't include Alonzo Church. In the classroom, things went much better. Between them they explored further into their answers to the *Entscheidungsproblem*, refining their joint thesis that's still the standard explanation to Hilbert's challenge. Turing also started work on a practical, working version of a primitive computing machine; when he returned to England in 1938 with his PhD he also took with him a circuit board holding three of the four necessary stages. His PhD dissertation had focused heavily on machine computing, including complex issues like the "halting problem". This was something he had first mentioned during his work at Cambridge. If a Turing Machine is set to work with a given set of inputs, is it possible to tell if it will ever come to the end of its program or keep running forever? Turing concluded that it isn't. At Princeton he introduced the idea of "oracles," additional processors that could answer this and many other problems. In some ways, his oracles were similar to a modern self-test program, but in 1938 they were definitely just mathematical models used to assist with advanced calculations. They weren't real.

By this time, however, Turing had another reason to work at turning his concepts into reality. Unknown to Church or anyone else at Princeton, before he traveled to the USA he had been discreetly approached by a shadowy British intelligence agency. They were interested in his work, and he'd quietly decided to cooperate with them. They were curious about the use of a real-life Turing Machine to solve certain specialized types of algorithms. It didn't take a brain as powerful as Turing's to work out what they meant; the organization went by the abbreviation GC&CS, which stood for Government Code and Cypher School.

After Princeton, Turing settled easily back into his old life at Cambridge. Once more he was in the secure environment of King's College, with the time and freedom to go on with his work. He marked essays, tutored undergraduates, tinkered with his prototype machine and ran endless miles through the flat Cambridgeshire countryside. He also sat through any lecture he thought might boost his already formidable knowledge of mathematics. Some of these were given by Ludwig Wittgenstein, an aristocratic Jewish Austrian who'd been at Cambridge on and off since 1912, fought for the Austro-Hungarian Empire during the First World War, then took British citizenship after the Nazis seized power in his native land. He'd been a Fellow of Trinity College since 1929, and became a professor of philosophy there in 1939. His specialty subjects included the logical basis of mathematics, and Turing was keen to hear his views on it. He was less keen when he heard them. Wittgenstein believed that mathematics could only invent concepts of use to mathematicians; Turing was convinced it could discover absolute truths about the world. The two discussed the issue, and then argued about it. Turing came away impressed with Wittgenstein's intellect, but remained convinced that his conclusions were wrong.

By September 1938, Turing was convinced that mathematics *had* to deliver absolute truths. On his return from Princeton he'd spoken to GC&CS again, and discussed what he'd learned in the USA. The British interest in breaking codes – cryptanalysis – was becoming urgent. In 1936, Nazi Germany had reoccupied the Rhineland, which had been demilitarized since the end of the First World War. Austria was annexed by Germany in March 1938. There was little protest and, encouraged by this success, Hitler began whipping up a crisis over the Sudetenland area of Czechoslovakia. This region was mostly populated by ethnic Germans, and they were keen to join the growing Third Reich, but the Czechoslovak government didn't want to lose territory. By late summer, Nazis in the Sudetenland were demanding union with Germany and the British prime minister, Neville Chamberlain, was involved in trying to negotiate a settlement. Chamberlain believed that by appeasing Hitler's demands – not all of which were unreasonable; the Rhineland had been thoroughly pillaged by France, for example – it would be possible to avoid another European war. Others in Britain were more realistic. A huge rearmament program was quietly getting into gear, and the military hoped appeasement would buy them enough time to be ready to fight. The top brass and intelligence agencies believed that war was now inevitable, and they wanted every advantage they could get. One vital edge would be the ability to read the enemy's signals, which the British had done successfully in the last war and wanted to repeat this time round.

But there was a problem.

CHAPTER 5: ENIGMA

Arthur Scherbius was born in Frankfurt-am-Main on October 20, 1878. At university in Munich and Hannover he studied the growing field of electricity, and was awarded a doctorate in electrical engineering in 1904. For the next fourteen years he led a competent but unremarkable career, designing turbines and coming up with the sort of eccentric inventions that were common in the early days of domestic power supply – he invented an electric pillow, for example. Then in February 1918 he founded his own company, Scherbius & Ritter, and patented a design for a machine that would easily encrypt sensitive messages. He offered to sell it to the German Navy and foreign office but they politely refused; they already had codes which, they were sure, were perfectly adequate (they weren't – the British were reading them). Soon the war ended and Germany didn't need codes any more, but in 1923 Scherbius and Ritter formed a new company, *Chiffriermaschinen Akten-Gesellschaft*, and started marketing an improved version to banks.

Some banks liked the idea of being able to send messages nobody could read, and Scherbius sold enough machines to keep the company afloat. New machines were developed and the original model – a monster that weighed well over 100 pounds – was refined into a device less than a quarter of the weight and small enough to be carried in a neat wooden case. Several hundred were exported; the German Navy bought a few and various diplomatic services tried them out. Then, on May 13, 1929, Scherbius stepped into the street without looking, and was fatally run down by a horse. In 1933, the Nazis came to power and began a huge, secret rearmament drive. Abruptly *Chiffriermaschinen Akten-Gesellschaft* stopped trading publicly, and the machines disappeared from the market.[ix] Out of the public eye, however, an expanded factory was gearing up to produce thousands of an even more sophisticated version. Scherbius had named his machine the Enigma, and had developed the commercial versions A to D. The pre-Nazi German army had adopted an upgraded one in 1928, the last Scherbius design, named the Enigma-G. These machines were hard, but not impossible, to defeat. This new version was for German military use only. It was called the Enigma-I, and it was a nightmare.

The Enigma-I, also known as the Service Enigma, came in a case eleven inches wide, just over a foot long and six inches high. Opening the top revealed a simple 26-key, typewriter-style keyboard in the German QWERTZ layout, with a matching panel of 26 labeled lamps above it.

Finally, there were three slots in the top casing, with the notched edge of a wheel projecting through each. Lowering the front of the box revealed a plugboard with 26 numbered double sockets, which could be joined together in pairs with short plug-tipped cables. The case was varnished wood with brass fittings, the body of the machine itself black-painted steel. Inside the lid were holders for spare plugboard cables, as well as paper notices with instructions on proper use and security. The steel casing of the machine itself contained a 4.5 volt battery and an electromechanical cypher machine of fiendish complexity.

The basic principle of a secret code is that the actual letters of a message – in what's known as the *cleartext* alphabet - are swapped for different, unrecognizable symbols in a *cyphertext* alphabet. Most children have played games involving simple codes. A familiar one is a stepping code; the cyphertext alphabet is simply the cleartext alphabet, but "stepped" a certain number of places along. Six steps would look like this:

ABCDEFGHIJKLMNOPQRSTUVWXYZ

GHIJKLMNOPQRSTUVWXYZABCDEF

Another common version is the keyword code; in this, a keyword that contains no repeated letters is chosen and used as the start of the cyphertext alphabet. If the chosen keyword was *cypher* it would look like this:

ABCDEFGHIJKLMNOPQRSTUVWXYZ

CYPHERABDFGIJKLMNOQSTUVWXZ

To encode a message all you have to do is match each letter of cleartext with the corresponding letter of cyphertext. Using the first code with a step of six, the message:

This is an encyphered message

Would become:

ZNOY OY GT KTIVNKXKJ SKMMGMK

To make it more difficult to guess individual words, and therefore learn some of the substitutions, it's a good idea to break the message into "words" of even length, say five characters:

ZNOYO YGTKT IVNKX KJSKM MGMK

A simple substitution cypher like this is enough to prevent a casual attacker from reading a message. It has a serious weakness, though, and will never resist an attack by a cryptanalyst – a codebreaker. That's because it's *monoalphabetic* – the same substitution is used for the entire message. Letters don't all occur at the same frequency; some are more common than others. In English, the most common letter by far is E. Looking at our sample message we can see that K appears five times, and no other letter appears more than three times. A cryptanalyst would guess that *K* corresponds to *E* – and it does. The same can be done with the other letters of the alphabet, although with decreasing accuracy as you work down the list, but for a message longer than about a hundred characters it's usually possible to get over half of them in this way. By that stage it's possible for intelligence analysts to guess the rest. Letter frequency is a weakness that affects all monoalphabetic cyphers; there's no way around it.

The next stage is to use a *polyalphabetic* cypher – one that uses multiple alphabets throughout the message. The most secure development of that is to use a different alphabet for every character. The first known example dates back to 1467 and used concentric disks with cleartext and cyphertext alphabets marked round the edges. The first character was encyphered, then the cyphertext disk was advanced one letter and the second character was encoded. This process was repeated for each letter, so every substitution was different and frequency analysis no longer worked. The problem was that both sender and receiver needed identical disk sets, and if an enemy got hold of the disk they could attack the cypher. They wouldn't know which starting position to use but 26 attempts would be enough to get it right, and after that they'd be able to read messages.

More complex polyalphabetic cyphers were developed over the next century, culminating in 1586 with the Vigenère Cypher. This used a grid of 26 alphabets, each one stepped by one place, which were used in a sequence determined by a keyword. It was thought to be unbreakable as late as the American Civil War and was used by the Confederate Army. In fact, Charles Babbage, the English computer pioneer, had quietly broken it in 1846. The USA managed to break the Confederate codes on a regular basis, because the keywords were easily guessed, but Babbage, a talented mathematician, had managed a true cryptanalytic attack. The weakness he had identified was that the key repeated at a set interval. If repeated words, or even parts of words, were encyphered at the same point in the alphabet sequence patterns began to emerge.

So polyalphabetic cyphers were far more secure than monoalphabetic ones, but unless the key repeat interval was very long they could still be broken. The problem was that creating and using such long keys was very difficult to do by hand. What Scherbius had invented, and the German Army had refined, was a machine that could generate an almost infinite number of polyalphabetic alphabets with a repeat interval that was truly staggering.

The heart of the Enigma machine is the keyboard. There's a key for each letter of the alphabet and they look just like the ones on an old-fashioned typewriter. They're quite stiff to push, though. That's because when a key is pressed it's not just flicking up a lightweight arm with a metal letter on the end. Instead, it does two things. Firstly, it moves a lever that connects to the rotors at the back of the case. Secondly, it closes a switch, activating the electric circuit for the chosen letter. A current passes through the machine and finally arrives at one of the 26 small lettered lamps – which one depends on the exact way the machine is set up – and illuminates it. The operator or an assistant writes down the letter of the lamp that lit up, then types the next letter and the process is repeated. From the outside it looks simple; in fact, it's anything but. Inside the machine, nine separate substitutions are carried out with each press of a key.

The Steckerbrett

When a key is pressed and the circuit closes, the flow of current from the battery first reaches the plugboard on the front of the machine. This was always called by its German name, *Steckerbrett*. It consists of 26 sockets, one for each letter of the alphabet and each consisting of a large and a slightly smaller hole. Short cables, with a two-pronged *Stecker* or plug at each end, can be used to connect these in pairs. If the operator presses E the current will reach the socket marked E, but that could be connected to any other letter or to none at all. If the socket is empty a sprung contact inside it sends the signal on as E. If it's "steckered" to R then R will be sent on. The machine came with twelve cables – ten for normal use and two spares. Strangely, the number of possible ways to set up the board is highest with eleven pairs of sockets connected; less or more will give fewer combinations. The Germans used ten for convenience. This gave three-quarters as many possible alphabets as eleven would have done – but the number was still over 150 million million. Of course it could still be broken by letter frequency analysis because once it was set up the same substitution would be used for each letter.

The Rotors

From the *Steckerbrett* the current goes on to the *Eintrittwalz*, the entry rotor. This is a fixed disk with 26 electrical contacts on its face; each one is connected to a socket on the board. To the left of it are three rotors. Each of them looks like a wheel with a notched, extended edge and a "tire" or ring marked with letters A-Z (Navy machines) or numbers 1-26 (Army and Air Force machines). There are 26 contacts on each side of the wheel, wired together in pairs – but not directly. The A contact on the right of the wheel isn't wired to the A contact on the left; it's connected to a different one. The original machine came with three rotors, each of which could be fitted in any position. Each machine had an identical set, and the rotors in a set were marked with Roman numerals – I, II and III. On rotor I, the A contact on the right is wired to the E contact on the left; B is wired to K, C to M and so on. For rotor II, the first three pairs are A-A, B-J and C-D. With three rotors they could be loaded into the machine in six different orders, and each rotor would carry out a separate substitution of the letter.

However, the outer rings complicate things. Each ring has a notch cut into its edge, and the ring can be rotated around the rotor to any of 26 positions. When the machine is set up the letters or numbers on the rings can be seen through three small windows in the casing, but if the letter A is visible there are still 26 different ways the rotor could be set up. With six possible rotor orders that means another 105,456 possible alphabets.

The Reflector

Once the current has passed through all three rotors it hits the reflector. This is another fixed wheel, and again it has 26 contacts on one side. These are wired together in pairs, so a current that comes in to the reflector through one contact goes out through another. There were two reflectors, each with different wiring, doubling the number of possible alphabets produced by the *Steckerbrett* and rotors.

When the current leaves the reflector it travels back through the rotors again, going through three more substitutions. Because it enters the row of rotors at a different contact, this time it follows a completely new path through them, before coming back out at a (different) contact on the *Eintrittswalz*. From there it goes back through the steckers – the ninth and last substitution – and finally to one of the lamps, which lights up a letter for the operator to write down. When the key is released the circuit breaks, the lamp goes out and the Enigma is ready for the next letter. But that next letter will not follow the same path through the machine.

The final, terrifyingly complex refinement of the Enigma machine is the system of levers that connects the keyboard to the rotors. As a key is pressed it moves a small steel pawl against the notched edge of the first rotor. That pawl turns the rotor one twenty-sixth of a revolution; then it stops and, as the operator presses the key all the way down, the circuit closes and lights up the lamp. When he types the next letter the rotor moves again, so when the circuit closes the six substitutions carried out by the rotors have changed. With the machine set up in one specific way, the operator could press E and the R lamp would light up. If he presses E again it might be G,

P, or in fact any letter except E. Every 26 keystrokes, a stud on the first rotor catches the notch on the second rotor's ring and turns that one position, too. If the message is long enough a stud on the second rotor turns the third.

Now letter frequency analysis won't work because the cypher is polyalphabetic, and repeat interval analysis won't work either because the intervals are so immense. With ten letter pairs steckered and a set of three rotors there are a lot of ways to set up the machine, *and the cypher changes every time a key is pressed.*

The British cryptanalysts were faced with an apparently impossible task. Each letter in an Enigma message was encyphered with a different alphabet, chosen by the machine from a vast array of options. For another German signaler, with another Enigma machine set up in exactly the same way as the one that had encyphered the message, turning it back into plaintext was a simple job. Without knowing how to set up the machine, though, the number of possible alphabets was staggering. In fact there were

107,458,491,300,000,000,000,000

of them. Faced with a number so frighteningly enormous the intelligence officers decided to do the only sensible thing. They asked a mathematician.

CHAPTER 6: FIGHTING THE ODDS

In fact, GC&CS weren't the first people to ask a mathematician to take a look at Scherbius's terrifying invention. The Polish Army were extremely worried about Hitler, who was loudly threatening to seize the regions of their country that had once been part of Germany, and they had been looking closely at Enigma for a long time. They began attacking the code in the 1920s, before the Nazis even came to power. On September 1, 1932 three mathematicians from Poznan University joined the Polish Cypher Bureau and were set to work on Enigma. Their names were Marian Rejewski, Henryk Zygalski and Jerzy Rózycki, and they deserve a lot more recognition than they've ever had.

In 1932, French military intelligence, who knew of the Polish project, passed on two stolen German military documents and two of the vital Enigma key sheets.

These sheets, as much as the machine itself, were at the heart of Enigma's power. The rotor order, ring settings and steckered letter pairs were collectively known as a key setting. For the system to work every machine on a radio net had to be set up with the same key setting, and to make that possible key sheets were distributed to every radio station. Each sheet contained the key settings to be used every day for a month.

The Poles, like many other governments, had bought commercial Enigmas from Scherbius in the 1920s. They knew the way the contacts in the rotors and reflector were paired. It was already obvious that the new military machines were wired differently, but they didn't know how. The material from the French changed all that. Through some brilliant calculations, Rejewski was able to use the key sheets and encyphered messages to work out the wiring inside each of the military wheels and reflectors. That let him build replicas of the machine. It didn't help him with breaking the code, though. Without the key setting a message was encoded with he'd have to set up the machine, type the first few characters and see if what came out was readable German text or gibberish. When that failed he'd have to change to a new setting, try again, and keep on going until clear text came out. That could mean trying a substantial fraction of all the machine's possible settings – and there were 107,458,491,300,000,000,000,000 of them.

Enigma is an old system now, and it has a flaw that's gained a lot of attention: it can never encypher a letter as itself. If you type E on the keyboard any of the lamps could light up *except* the E lamp. This is an unavoidable problem with rotor machines that use a reflector and it is, technically, a weakness. It's not a significant one, though; used properly, Enigma was very secure indeed. In fact, it's *still* very secure indeed. In modern terms, a standard Enigma-I machine has a "key strength" equivalent to 76-bit encryption, which an organization like the National Security Agency could crack through a brute force attack, using supercomputers to test every possible combination until clear text emerges. Even with multiple Cray YMPs working on the code, though, it could take two or three days. The U-Boat Enigma M4 gave 84-bit encryption; the NSA might need a couple of *years* to get into that. Breaking Enigma by brute force is a challenge now, and in 1939, it was utterly unthinkable. On the other hand, Enigma enthusiasts regularly manage to break original wartime messages in a couple of days on a home PC.[x] How?

The answer is simple. They don't begin with a brute force attack; they use a variety of techniques to drastically narrow the options first. That's what the Poles (and later the British) did, too. Mathematics alone wasn't enough; breaking Enigma was going to take a blend of mathematics and cunning.

The Polish trio left the machine itself for a while and concentrated on studying how it was used. They were hoping to find weaknesses in the German procedures, and slowly hints began to accumulate. Many German operators were careless and there were flaws in the operating instructions, too. Every day's key settings included three letters – the *Grundstellung* – that decided the start position of the rotors. With the machine set up those letters showed in the three windows. The sender would then choose three new letters and encrypt them on the machine, send them, then reset the machine to those three letters and type the rest of the message. The receiver would decrypt the letters, set them on his machine and decode the message. The Germans made a massive mistake, though. To prevent errors caused by bad radio reception they ordered this encrypted wheel start position to be sent *twice*. The first six letters of an Enigma message was actually the same three letters, repeated. When the Poles found out, they realized that, while the first and fourth, second and fifth and third and sixth letters of the message were different in cyphertext, *in plaintext they were the same letter.*

This wasn't like the reflector issue, a theoretical fault that in reality was nowhere near as bad as it sounds. This really *was* a weakness, and it was a serious one. Because they knew the rotor wiring, they could deduce just enough information to start reconstructing the key setting and eliminate a huge percentage of the possible settings for that day. There were still hundreds of thousands of possibilities, but the number was now small enough that a skilled mathematician could attack it. Rejewski built up a card index of identified patterns in the six-letter groups that could tell him which rotors were being used and in which order, and designed a machine to speed up the process. By the time he was done, he could identify the day's rotor order in less than fifteen minutes. He still didn't know the stecker connections or ring settings, but that didn't matter much. With the key element of the constantly stepping rotors neutralized Enigma was reduced to a very complex monoalphabetic cypher, and frequency analysis could break that.

Then, in November 1937, he found himself suddenly shut out. It was the first sign of a problem that would torment cryptanalysts all the way to the end of the war. Enigma was a moving target; the Germans kept having new ideas to make it even more secure. Because the machine was modular this was very easy for them to do. The simplest way was simply to make extra components, and that's what they'd just done. Up to now, every machine was supplied with a single reflector. Now a second, differently wired, one was issued, and the key setting was expanded to say which one was to be used that day. When Rejewski guessed what had happened he started building a new index for the new reflector, which took almost a year. By then there were other problems.

In fact there were already other problems. The *Kriegsmarine*, the German Navy, always had the tightest procedures for using Enigma and for long periods its traffic couldn't be read at all. In May 1937 they'd stopped encoding simple text messages and switched to a code book system. Standard formats were developed for every kind of message that could be sent – contact reports, weather updates, changes of course and many more. These formats were filled out using four-number code groups that each represented a common word or phrase. *"Enemy in sight"* was no longer written as *"Feind in sicht"* – now it became 0292.[xi] These numbers were converted to letters with a simple substitution code, then enciphered on Enigma. Even if a cryptanalyst managed to get the right key settings their replica machine would still spit out gibberish – *they wouldn't be able to tell that they'd broken the code.*

Army and Air Force signals also went dark, in May 1938. The Germans had changed the procedure; now operators chose a new *Grundstellung* for each message and sent that first. This problem wasn't as serious, though. Many of the operators were lazy and chose the same three letters for every message; one famous operator had a girlfriend called Cilli, and set his machine to CIL every time. Careless mistakes like this made the Poles' job much easier. Meanwhile, Henryk Zygalski had come up with a new tool.

Sometimes, in about 12 per cent of messages, one of the pairs in the vital first six characters would contain the same letter twice. Zygalski nicknamed this a *Female*, because while men have an X and a Y chromosome women have a double X. If the first six letters of a message were KXLQXM then the 2nd and 5th letters – which were the same in plaintext – would be XX. Since the Poles knew the rotor and reflector wiring, that gave them another way in. He made up 26 large sheets, each marked with letters and punched with a pattern of holes. Each sheet represented a possible start position for the first rotor. When arranged in a stack and carefully moved in a set pattern, they simulated the settings of the machine. At first, many letters on the lower sheets would be visible through the holes on the top one. As the pattern progressed, if Zygalski had made the right guesses, the number of letters would decrease until only one remained. That would be the start position of the first rotor. Because only some start positions could produce females, and they were recorded in Rejewski's catalog, the rotor order of the machine could be deduced from that. Then frequency analysis could work out the steckering and the day's key was broken.

There was a big problem, though. A different stack of sheets was needed for each of the six possible rotor orders and, with limited resources, the team had to make them themselves. That meant getting the sheets printed then cutting out all the holes, which needed to be incredibly precise, with a razor blade. By mid-December 1938, Zygalski had only managed to complete two of the six sets he needed. Then disaster struck.

On December 15 the Germans introduced two new rotors, IV and V. Now each daily key setting used three out of five, not three out of three. Six possible rotor orders became 60, and 60 sets of sheets were now needed. Zygalski had been working on his sheets for weeks and had done a third of the job; now the size of the task was clearly impossible. Dispirited, the Poles switched their hopes to Rejewski's latest idea. He had decided that as the German cypher was created by a machine, perhaps it could be broken by a machine. His invention contained six triple drums, each wired to simulate an Enigma rotor stack. Like the Zygalski sheets it relied on females to find the key setting, but where the sheets needed ten females from a day's messages to reliably break the key, the new machine only needed three. The detected females would be set on the machine using plugs, it was switched on, then each of its drums tested one of the six possible rotor orders until a circuit was made. At that point, electromagnets would stop the spinning drums with a loud bang, the settings it had stopped at would be read off and the key was broken. The design of the machine reduced the options to 17,576 and it could test them all in a couple of hours. For long-forgotten reasons – perhaps the bang it made when it stopped, perhaps because it resembled a popular ice cream dish of the time – it was nicknamed the *bomba kryptologiczna;* the "cryptologic bomb." Rejewski had one running by October 1938 and it was a great success.

Then came the new rotors.

Rejewski was able to work out the wiring of the two new rotors within a few weeks because the SD, the intelligence agency of the SS, hadn't updated its procedures and still used the same *Grundstellung* for all of a day's messages. That wasn't a huge help, however, because the number of possible settings had still increased by a factor of ten. Now, to test all 60 possible rotor orders, ten *bombas* would be needed. The Poles set to work building them, but by July 1939 they had only completed four, and the political situation was going downhill rapidly. War with Germany was likely within weeks. At that point, they decided to ask for help.

Up to now Poland's British and French allies had known that the Poles were trying to break Enigma. They didn't know that breaks had been achieved. Now the Poles called a secret conference and asked for the leading French and British cryptanalysts to attend. The leader of the British delegation was Alfred Dillwyn "Dilly" Knox, an irritable genius who'd worked as a code breaker for Naval Intelligence during the First World War. Knox was a legend among British cryptanalysts, partly because he'd helped break the "Zimmerman Telegram" whose revelations of German treachery had brought the USA into the war in 1917. Knox had already met the Poles in January 1939, although they hadn't revealed their successes then. He had impressed them with his obvious knowledge of Enigma, and now they asked him to come to their conference. Knox agreed, and travelled to Warsaw on July 26. With him he brought a paper slide rule he'd developed which could break any Enigma model without a plugboard, including those used by the Spanish fascists, the Italian navy and the German secret service. He also brought Alan Turing.

Perhaps because he was a mathematician himself (Knox was an expert on ancient Egyptian scrolls), Turing was extremely impressed by the work the three young Poles had done. He had investigated some aspects of the Enigma that the Poles had overlooked, and he now passed this knowledge on, but he also had a lot to learn from them and he soaked it up eagerly. What he was less impressed by was their limited resources. Turing had been working part-time for GC&CS since September 1938 and he was very aware of the urgency. Now he was appalled that Zygalski had to produce his sheets by hand in such a slow and inefficient way. When the conference ended the formula for the sheets was among the package of material the Poles handed over to Knox, and as soon as he arrived back in England, Turing swung into action. A printer's shop capable of perforating paper sheets was found and sworn to secrecy, sixty sets of sheets were run off and a printing press fitted with a perforator stamped down on each one, cutting out the appropriate holes. Within days, Turing had achieved what Zygalski had struggled with for months. The thick bundle of sheets didn't go straight to Warsaw, though. First it was taken to an ugly mansion in a small English town.

Turing

CHAPTER 7: BLETCHLEY PARK

When Knox worked for Naval Intelligence in the First World War, they'd been based in the Admiralty Building in London, in an office that became famous as Room 40. It was obvious that this war would be different, though. The bombardment of the Spanish city Guernica in 1937 had shown that the Nazis had a powerful bomber force and wouldn't hesitate to use it against towns and cities. London's Whitehall district, packed with government and military offices, would be an obvious target. If crypt-analysis was going to be a vital weapon against the Reich's military power the codebreakers needed to be kept safe, so a new location had to be found. There was also a suspicion that the volume of traffic Enigma could generate would need more than a dozen people with pencils and paper sitting in a big office. In 1938, a team began looking for a country estate they could discreetly buy, and before long attention began to focus on Bletchley Park.

The town of Bletchley, fifty miles north of London, is now part of the post-War "New Town" of Milton Keynes. Before being abruptly reduced to neighborhood status by the planners in 1967 it had existed since at least the 12th century. In 1845 it was a tiny village, but the opening of the London and North West Railway that year boosted its importance. Soon, the town's station was the meeting point of four major rail lines and dozens of trains a day passed through. The building boom of the Victorian period then helped Bletchley expand again. The growing town was built on heavy clay soil and it soon became a manufacturing center for bricks. Today the area is dotted with artificial lakes formed when the old clay pits flooded. By 1938, Bletchley was a typical small industrial town, dominated by the kilns and chimneys of the brickworks, and coated in a light film of soot from the trains on the LNWR line.

Near the southeast corner of Bletchley, 400 yards from the rail yards and station, stands a large house. Surrounded by 580 acres of farmland, meadows and woods, there's been a house on that spot since the Domesday Book was compiled nearly a thousand years ago. This house was built in 1883, and almost everyone agrees that it's hideous. With all the elaborate decoration of a typical Victorian mansion but none of the elegance, nothing about the house - an unfortunate mix of honey-colored stone and local red brick – looks right. Its last resident had sold up in 1937; the new owner planned to demolish the lot and develop the area as housing – or so he said. In fact, the syndicate of property developers who'd bought the estate was led by a Captain Faulkner of Naval Intelligence. His former boss, Admiral Sir Hugh Sinclair, was now the chief of MI6 and was fed up waiting for the government to find a new home for GC&CS. He sent Faulkner to bid on the house at auction, paid for it himself and turned it over to the codebreakers.[xii] Then, while Sinclair argued with the government to get his money back, GC&CS moved in.

The residents of Bletchley had been expecting to see the bulldozers arrive to flatten the old house; instead, it was opened up again and "Captain Ridley's shooting party" began roaming the grounds. In fact, they were carefully surveying the property, working out how many people it could hold and how to expand it into a codebreaking operation on an industrial scale. Soon Post Office engineers arrived too, discreetly installing a mass of new telephone lines to connect the old house to London and the nation's leaders.

By late August 1939, any hope of avoiding a war had vanished. Bletchley Park now became the official home of GC&CS, and personnel started to arrive. Germany invaded Poland on September 1, provoking Neville Chamberlain's fateful ultimatum to Hitler: withdraw or else. Hitler, who understandably had a low opinion of the western Allies' resolve - after all, they'd done nothing when he'd taken over the Rhineland, Austria, the Sudetenland and then the rest of Czechoslovakia – airily dismissed it as a bluff. But this time it was no bluster. Chamberlain had at last realized how dangerous Hitler was and his threat was, finally, for real. On September 3, German troops were still advancing into Poland, brutally sweeping away all resistance as they went. That evening,

Chamberlain announced that Britain was now at war with Germany. Similar declarations immediately followed from the major British Empire nations and from France. The next day staff began arriving at Bletchley Park, and within hours "Station X" was operational.

Station X was run by the chief of GC&CS, Royal Navy Commander Alistair Denniston. Denniston had worked with Knox in Room 40 during the First World War; now he was in charge of Britain's entire cryptanalysis effort. Knox was responsible for the attack on Enigma. To assist him, Turing arrived on September 4, along with another Cambridge mathematician, Gordon Welchman. They had the Polish tools at their disposal, including one of Rejewski's replica Enigmas, but progress was slow and for months, no messages were broken. On September 17, the USSR invaded Poland from the east and the Polish Cypher Bureau, suddenly finding their Warsaw base in immediate danger, escaped south through Romania – the two countries shared a border at the time – and made their way to France. Rejewski, Zygalski and Ró-zycki were soon at work at PC Bruno, a signal intercept station near Paris. PC Bruno quickly established a direct telegraph cable to Bletchley Park and the two stations worked closely together for the next nine months. Ironically, the message traffic was secured by the replica Enigmas – but with Rejewski at one end and Turing at the other, their encryption procedures had none of the errors that plagued the Germans.

The Poles had managed the first effective breaks into the steckered German Enigma before the war, but Turing and Knox were worried. All the Polish methods relied on a single weakness: the German practice of sending the message key twice. At any time, the Germans might realize the vulnerability this caused, and change their procedures. It was essential to find a more robust method of breaking the code.

The Poles had looked at the Enigma's reflector design, and were aware that while it wasn't a major fault it could be exploited in some circumstances. In the end, they'd gone with the message key vulnerability, because it was easier. Now Turing and Welchman went back and looked again. Normally, the fact that the machine could never encipher a message as itself didn't matter much, but if the cryptanalyst knew or could guess part of the plaintext, things changed slightly. If a known or guessed piece of plaintext could be slid along the line of cyphertext, any position where the two had matching letters could be ruled out. That would leave a much smaller number of positions where the plaintext and cyphertext might match.

By this time the Enigma had 1,074,584,913,000,000,000,000,000 possible key settings, but starting with the same piece of cyphertext they would all create different cyphertexts. If the British had part of the message, they could use that to identify the only key setting that could have produced it, then set up their own machine with that key and decode the whole message. Known or guessed plaintext was added to Bletchley Park's growing specialist jargon; it became known as a "crib".

Of course, there was still a problem. If Bletchley had a crib and an intercepted message only one key setting could have produced one from the other, but which one?

There were 1,074,584,913,000,000,000,000,000 possibilities, after all. What was needed was a way to check them all very quickly. Turing still had his full set of Zygalski sheets at the time, but they were obviously too slow. Now his thoughts turned to the *bomba* Rejewski had shown him in July. With his own interest in computing machines, the device had an obvious appeal for him despite its limitations. Of course, a real Turing machine would be programmable to solve any problem, but the technology to build one didn't exist yet. Here was something that *could* be built, though – a machine designed to solve one clearly defined problem.

Turing had only been at Bletchley a matter of days before he began sketching out his design. He wanted to avoid the main weakness of the *bomba*, its reliance on the repeated message key, and design something that could attack messages using just a crib. He also wanted it to be much, much faster; the *bomba* could break the key in a couple of hours when only three rotors were available, but that became almost a day now there were five. His solution was a radical step forwards. Once the concept was complete a proper design had to be produced from it; Turing was a mathematician, not an engineer.

Again, they got lucky. Someone remembered that the British Tabulating Machine Company was based in Letchworth, 20 miles away. BTM had been set up to sell electromechanical adding machines, first imported ones made by the US Tabulating Machine Company (which changed its name to IBM in 1924) and then later its own designs. The basic technology was similar, so BTM chief engineer Harold "Doc" Keen was brought in to turn Turing's sketches into reality.

Rejewski's *bomba* with its six drums was a relatively small machine that sat comfortably on a table. Turing's bombe was a monster. Seven feet wide, two feet deep and six and a half feet high, it weighed over a ton and contained 111 drums – 36 three-drum scramblers and a set of three indicator drums to show possible settings. Each of the scramblers mimicked an Enigma machine and the drums themselves, color-coded to show which Enigma rotor they emulated, could be placed on any of each scrambler's three axles. Simulated reflectors were built in to each end of the bombe casing and a mass of 26-way cables at the rear made it easy to quickly reconfigure. Cribs were turned into "menus" that were set on the huge machine through a plugboard; more plugboards allowed it to test not just rotor orders, but stecker connections too. The bombe was electrically powered and the top drums – matching the Enigma's "fast" right rotor – turned at 50.4 rpm. With 26 combinations checked in each revolution of the drum that meant each scrambler could test 22 key settings every second, and there were 36 of them. Stuttering and clattering, humming with electricity and spraying a faint mist of oil in every direction,[xiii] the whole bombe could check 792 keys a second; 47,520 in a minute; nearly six million in the time it took Rejewski's machine to check 17,526.

It was still too slow.

The first bombe, named Victory, was delivered to the Park on March 18, 1940. Even before it arrived, Turing and Keen were working on plans for an improved version that would run the "fast" rotors at 120rpm, boosting its operating speed to 1,872 keys per second. They also found another problem, however. Like its Polish counterpart, the bombe tested each possible key by trying to run an electric current through the scrambler. If there was no circuit the scrambler kept clicking round; if a circuit was made, the machine thudded to a halt and the operator would read the solution off the indicator drums. Each solution was then examined for logical contradictions by a cryptanalyst, and if it passed that test it was set up on a replica Enigma and tested on a message. If nonsense came out, the bombe was restarted; if German text emerged, the key was broken. The problem was that, unless the bombe had a very long crib to work with – up to 150 letters – it produced a huge number of false stops. Testing all of these strained even Bletchley's resources.

Then Gordon Welchman stepped in and suggested an improvement. He designed an attachment for the bombe that used the fact that stecker connections were symmetrical – if A was steckered to B then B was steckered to A – to eliminate huge numbers of false stops. With this device, known as the *diagonal board*, fitted, the required crib length dropped dramatically. Now the cryptanalysts were looking for cribs of twelve letters or more, but if necessary they could run the bombe with eight.

In January 1940, while BTM were building the first bombe, Turing had visited the Poles at CP Bruno. He gave them the set of Zygalski sheets he'd had made the year before, and discussed their progress. On January 17, Zygalski and Rejewski achieved the first break of a wartime Enigma message, although it was an old one from

October 1939. From then, through the first half of 1940, CP Bruno was breaking around 17 per cent of all Enigma messages cracked by the Allies. It was a good performance considering their limited resources, but Turing could see the writing on the wall. Their methods were ingenious but fragile; it couldn't last.

On May 10, 1940, the Germans launched a huge offensive through Holland, Belgium and Luxembourg, aimed at outflanking the French border defenses. Nobody saw it coming, because just before the panzers started to roll the *Wehrmacht*'s message traffic suddenly went dark; the breaks into Enigma stopped abruptly. What Turing had feared was now reality: the Germans had changed their message key procedure and all of the Polish techniques were suddenly useless. It was time to spin up the bombe in earnest.

CHAPTER 8: BLITZKRIEG

The French Army and the British Expeditionary Force
had been expecting an attack and had been aware that
German forces might come through Belgium. However,
there was a curious blind spot in French and British
(and later US) military thinking about Belgium's hilly,
heavily-wooded Ardennes region. It was believed that
the terrain was too poor to move large forces through it
quickly, despite the fact that the Germans had done exactly that in 1870, 1914 and 1917. Now, in 1940, they did it
again.[2] If the Germans did come that way, France's de-
fenders believed, the Belgian Army's resistance would
buy them several weeks to prepare strong defenses in
front of the advance.

---

[2] They would do it yet again in 1944, in the famous Battle of the
Bulge, surprising US troops who believed it would be a quiet sec-
tor.

They were badly wrong. Led by the hard-charging panzer generals Rommel and Guderian, the lead German units entered Belgium on May 10. By May 14 they had smashed through all resistance, and major fighting was taking place on French soil. Only three weeks later panzers were heading for Paris. With the Wehrmacht days away, PC Bruno abandoned its operations and the staff scattered. By the time Paris fell on June 14, Rejewski and Zygalski had escaped to the south of France with many of the French cryptanalysts. Finally, they made their way to neutral Spain, and from there caught ships to Britain. They were damaged goods, though. Because they'd spent time in Vichy France, the "free zone" controlled by French fascists, none of them were fully trusted. The two Poles were recruited into the Free Polish Army and set to work breaking hand-cyphered SS and SD codes, but they were never allowed near Bletchley Park. The Polish contribution to the war against Enigma was over. The British cryptanalysts were on their own.

They'd been expecting it, though, and they were as ready as they could be. Turing had managed another brilliant leap forward, eliminating many more of the possible key settings for each day's traffic. He had realized that, although each message was sent using a different start position, sometimes the rotors from one message would cycle through the start position of another. To detect this, he set up a system to punch received messages into special long index cards. By overlaying the cards on a light table, repeated sequences could be found. The cards, which were several yards long, were named "Banburies" after the town where they were made. One of Turing's many eccentricities was a habit of using German word endings, so this technique became known as *Banburismus*. It helped the bombe to work even faster.

In August 1940, a second bombe was completed, with Welchman's diagonal board installed, and the first one was returned to the factory to have the board fitted. The timing was ideal, because the Battle of Britain was raging as the Germans tried to bomb first the Royal Air Force, then London, into submission. Bletchley had made its first breaks into German Air Force messages in May, and by August they were reading them regularly – in fact, the Park's air intelligence office usually expected the daily key to be broken by breakfast time. That meant the British often knew the targets of the next day's air raids and could position their fighter squadrons to meet them. Bletchley also managed to collect valuable information about the strength of the German air force. That encouraged Churchill's defiance, because it turned out Hitler didn't have as many bombers as the RAF had feared.

Later that year Bletchley scored another major goal. Since the retreat from France in June Britain had feared an invasion, and the Wehrmacht had been collecting barges along the Channel ports in preparation for a crossing. As the summer's ferocious raids failed to win air superiority over the Channel, much less over southern England, the planned invasion was repeatedly postponed. Then, in September, the bombes spat out the cleartext of a message from Hitler. Air transport units based at Dutch airfields were ordered to stop their preparations for an air landing and dismantle their equipment. The intelligence staff quickly realized the importance of that. The invasion had been cancelled at least until 1941. In fact the plan would never be reactivated; by early the next year the fickle dictator's attention had turned east, to what would become the graveyard of his Thousand Year Reich - Russia.

The end of the invasion threat didn't mean the war was quietening down, though. Air raids continued, hammering ports and cities most nights. Savage battles were fought between the air forces and navies of both sides in an attempt to gain dominance over the Channel and North Sea. The war in North Africa began to heat up. And, out in the Atlantic, a new campaign was developing that was to bring Britain closer to defeat than at any other time.

CHAPTER 9: THE GRAY WOLVES

Germany's navy had been severely limited by the Treaty of Versailles that ended the First World War, including a ban on building submarines. However a covert submarine design office was set up in the Netherlands and when Hitler came to power there were already some advanced designs ready to be built. The Nazi dictator soon started finding ways to get round the treaty restrictions, such as building a limited number of U-Boats for "research" or "training" purposes, and before long was flouting them openly. By the beginning of the war the *Kriegsmarine* had a fleet of 65 U-Boats and the number was growing rapidly.

Early in the war it was dangerous for a U-Boat to even get to the Atlantic; the Royal Navy still controlled the English Channel and North Sea, and several submarines were sunk as they tried to break through. The fall of

France changed everything though. Massive bomb-proof U-Boat pens were built around the Bay of Biscay, and from these bases the boats could sail directly out into the open ocean. Because they were now 450 miles further west they could also range further into the Atlantic and stay on patrol for longer. With Britain relying heavily on shipments of fuel, food and raw materials from the Empire and the USA that was potentially disastrous. The Royal Navy's anti-submarine ships were fitted with the best sonar system in the world – ASDIC – but it could only detect submarines within 2,000 yards of the ship. It was excellent for pinning down and attacking a U-Boat that had already been detected visually or on radar, but it didn't have the range to search 41 million square miles of ocean for a small, quiet boat. Churchill pinned his hopes on Bletchley Park being able to find the prowling U-Boats by intercepting and reading their messages. The problem was that those messages were encyphered with the *Kriegsmarine*'s ultra-secure key settings.

Luckily Turing was already researching the Naval Enigma. His reason, typically, was "No-one else was doing anything about it and I could have it to myself."[xiv] Starting with work done by the Poles he managed to work out the very different and much more complex message key procedures that were being used. The standard naval machine was known as the M3, but it was identical to the Enigma-I apart from having letters on the rotor rings instead of numbers, and the rotors themselves were wired the same way. It wasn't long before he made an appalling discovery. The Poles had been locked out of German traffic when two extra rotors had been added, bringing the total to five. Now Turing discovered that the *Kriegsmarine* had issued an additional *three*, numbered VI, VII and VIII. This increased the possible rotor orders from 60 to 336 and the possible key settings to 6,017,675,512,800,000,000,000,000.

That might have been the end of the battle against the Naval Enigma right there, and could have changed the entire course of the war. The situation was subtly different, though. On land, Enigma machines were held at regimental and division headquarters and on *Luftwaffe* air bases, and with the Germans advancing everywhere there was little chance of these being captured. At sea, however, Britain was still dominant. The Royal Navy was the most powerful in the world until the US Navy overtook it in late 1943 and German ships were taking a risk if they went to sea. Many of them didn't get away with it, and the RN were under strict instructions to board German ships every chance they got and recover cryptographic material. Bletchley called these recoveries "pinches" and they were immensely helpful. Pinches could be people as well as material. One captured radio operator confirmed that numbers were now spelled out as text. Turing's new Naval Enigma section, Hut 8, analyzed every plaintext German naval message they had and found that over 90 per cent of them contained the number 1, written as EINS. They built a database of how EINS enciphered at every single rotor setting of the M3 Enigma – all 105,456 of them – and started using a BTM calculating machine to look for these settings in every naval message. Usually the steckering disguised it, but every so often E, I, N and S were all left unsteckered and the characters would match. There were many false matches too, but roughly one in four turned out to be real. When that happened, Hut 8 knew the rotor order, ring setting and start position, and only the steckering still had to be broken.

Banburismus also helped. Naval message keys were disguised using a simple substitution code based on a bigram table, which Turing slowly rebuilt using some clues and lots of calculations. When the table was rebuilt, Banburismus could reduce the 336 possible rotor orders to about 18, simplifying the bombe menus by a factor of 20.

One major problem was that the wiring of the three extra naval rotors was unknown. Then, on February 12, patrol ship HMS *Gleaner* surprised U-33 laying mines off the Scottish coast. She hammered the submarine with depth charges for several hours and finally managed to force her to the surface. The boat's crew set the self-destruct charges and prepared to abandon her, but the officers were worried that the British would manage to salvage the Enigma. There wasn't time to dismount the machine from the radio desk inside the smoke-filled, leaking hull, but the precious rotors were lifted out and distributed among three crewmen who were ordered to swim away from the sinking boat then drop them in the sea before they were rescued by the British. Two of them did so. The third, Friedrich Kumpf, did not. Panicking and almost overcome with hypothermia he was dragged aboard *Gleaner* and taken below to warm up. It was only when he began to recover that he remembered the rotors and urgently told one of the officers that he'd forgotten to ditch them. The officer checked Kumpf's pants, which were hanging up to dry, but the pockets were empty. The British had three of the rotors, including VI and VII.[xv]

On April 26, a German armed trawler was captured by HMS *Griffin*; the Enigma machine went over the side before *Griffin*'s marines could board her, but they captured an instruction manual and some decoded messages. Almost immediately they managed to break six days' worth of traffic.

These pinches and Turing's mathematical work allowed slow progress to be made on the M3 code, but out in the Atlantic, the situation was becoming desperate. The men of the *U-Boot-Waffe* called the period from June 1940 to April 1941 the Happy Time; their boats could roam undetected over most of the Atlantic and strike the vital supply convoys almost at will. In June, 284,113 tons of shipping went down to U-Boat attacks. In July it was a smaller but still disastrous 195,825 tons. Then, the figures began to creep remorselessly upwards: 267,618 tons in August, 293,335 in September. Britain controlled a third of the world's merchant shipping, but at this rate even that huge fleet couldn't survive for long. Bletchley had to break into M3. In early September, Lieutenant Commander Ian Fleming, who would later create James Bond, came up with a wild scheme to seize a German patrol boat with all its signals equipment intact. A captured German bomber would be deliberately crashed in the Channel with a crew of disguised commandos. When the Germans sent out a rescue boat, the assault squad would kill the crew and sail the boat back to England. For a variety of sensible reasons the plan was cancelled, but when Turing and assistant Peter Twinn heard the bad news they looked like "undertakers cheated of a nice corpse".[xvi] In October, 352,407 tons of shipping was lost to U-Boats.

Then came a brief respite. As the winter storms swept over the ocean, the submarine threat receded. U-Boats at sea spent much of their time just trying to survive, and it was far more difficult for them to detect a convoy visually and close to attack range. Losses fell slightly: 146,613 tons in November, 212,590 in December, "only" 126,782 in January 1941. Turing knew it would start to rise again as the weather improved, but then on March 4, commandos raided a German base on the Lofoten Islands. During the attack they captured the armed trawler *Krebs* and a complete set of naval rotors. They also found the key setting sheet for February, which should have been destroyed – in fact these sheets were printed with the days in reverse order, so that as soon as a day ended, its key could be cut off the bottom of the sheet and burned. In a rare example of naval carelessness, the captain of the *Krebs* hadn't done this. Turing now had everything he needed to complete his bigram table and upgrade the bombes to mimic rotor VIII. Suddenly, the messages started to break. Hut 8 had been running normal working hours, but now it switched to three shifts and a dedicated Crib Room was set up.

The work at the Park was long and stressful, but at the same time the station had developed something of the pre-War university atmosphere. There were many talented musicians among the staff, and they fitted in impromptu concerts around their shifts. The chess club thrived, and not surprisingly many of its members – Turing among them – were extremely good players. Eccentricity was also tolerated. Dilly Knox occasionally arrived at work in his pajamas. One cryptanalyst from the Japanese Section used to swim naked in the ornamental lake in front of the mansion. Turing stayed decently clothed, but still managed to stand out as more eccentric than most. He was nicknamed "the Prof" for his absent-minded academic manner, and his often elaborate solutions to minor problems. Crockery was always in short supply through the war, and theft of mugs was a common problem. Most people took care never to leave theirs unattended; Turing chained his to the radiator in Hut 8 and secured it with a massive padlock. When he had to go to meetings in London he often ran the fifty miles to Whitehall, a spectacular demonstration of his physical fitness, but for shorter trips around the Park or to the bombe stations he cycled. His bicycle was as eccentric as he was; after a certain number of revolutions the chain would jump off the sprocket. Turing studied the problem and worked out the interval, then counted his pedal strokes as he cycled. Just before the chain fell off he would sharply spin the pedals in reverse, retensioning it. Perhaps it never occurred to him to simply buy a new chain – or perhaps he saw advantages in a bike that would fall apart if anyone else tried to use it.[xvii] In early summer each year, he would suffer a severe attack of hay fever. Like everyone in Britain, he'd been issued a gas mask when war broke out and he found that it blocked pollen very effectively, although it did cause alarm and then hilarity.

People laughed at "the Prof" and his amusing quirks, but every day, around the clock, the work went on. Nobody doubted that it was deadly serious and absolutely vital.

On April 9, 1942, HMS *Aubretia*, HMS *Bulldog* and HMS *Broadway* hunted down U-110, which they knew had been damaged in a previous attack, and forced her to the surface 400 miles west of Iceland. This time, the boarding party recovered all the crypto material, including the complete M3 Enigma, key settings for the month and code books, as well as backup hand code sheets.[3] The submarine sank next day as the British were towing it to Scapa Flow in the Orkney Islands, but its signal room had already been stripped bare.

As soon as the captured sailors wrote home through the Red Cross, the Germans would have known that the keys for April might be in British hands, but they would have disregarded it. German cryptanalysts were well aware that Enigma could theoretically be broken, but didn't believe anyone would ever make the massive effort required. Their high command was simply convinced that it was unbreakable. The British might be able to read the traffic for April, they would have reasoned, but in May new key settings would kick in and the system would be secure again. They didn't know that Turing now had four bombes, all capable of attacking the M3, and that a growing percentage of traffic was being broken by the endlessly spinning machines.

Within weeks, the work began to pay off. Shipping losses in May and June were among the worst of the war – over 300,000 tons both months – but then they suddenly plunged. In July the submarines got 94,209 tons; in August only 80,310. Among the documents captured from U-110 was the critical Short Signal Book, which contained the code numbers the U-Boats were transmitting instead of words and phrases. With that they could generate cribs, despite the obscurity of the codes. That

---

[3] The controversial movie U-571 was loosely based on this incident.

was where Turing's Crib Room came into its own. By this time, the UK was dotted with signal intercept stations like Beaumanor or Chicksands (which was also a USAF intercept station during the Cold War, and is now the home of Britain's Intelligence Corps). These didn't just listen to the messages; they measured their bearings with direction-finding gear, too. If two or more stations picked up the same message the intersecting bearings would give a rough location for the U-Boat. If the U-Boat was near a convoy, the Crib Room could guess that the message was a sighting report. Based on the ships the U-Boat would have sighted – information that Bletchley knew – they could make a good guess at the contents of the message. That would be their crib, and it could then be checked with the Banburies and loaded onto a bombe. There was a good chance that, an hour later, that day's key would be broken.

Of course, Bletchley Park had to be careful. From their intercepts they knew where the U-Boats were, where their HQ had ordered them to be, and what condition the boats were in. It would have been easy to simply send a bomber or destroyer to each reported location and inflict heavy casualties on the U-Boat arm in a rapid series of attacks. The victory would have been short-lived, though. Every intelligence organization faces the dilemma of how to use the information it collects – exploiting it too obviously can tell the enemy what has happened, and if the Germans had ever known that Enigma was being broken they could have rapidly upgraded their security. In fact, when the British were hunting the German battleship *Bismarck* in May 1941 they faced exactly this problem. The ship had fought a series of battles against the Royal Navy, sinking the battlecruiser HMS *Hood* and damaging a British battleship, then slipped away into the Atlantic. She had taken damage herself, though, and the captain decided to head for occupied France. The RN had thrown massive forces into the chase, and on May 26, Turing's team broke a message from the battleship informing naval HQ that she was turning towards Brest - and giving her current location. However, *Bismarck* had broken contact with the pursuing ships the day before, and if she was suddenly attacked again the Germans might guess that her radio message had given her away. Instead, a squadron of PBY Catalina patrol planes was launched from Northern Ireland, to "search" the area and "find" the battleship. In fact, the planes' crews believed the search was genuine, but the Park already knew what they would find.[xviii] At 10:30am on May 26, Ensign Leonard B. Smith, a US Navy pilot who'd delivered his PBY to the UK then unofficially stayed on to fly for the RAF, sighted the *Bismarck*. Hours later, the final battle began as torpedo bombers and then battleships closed in from all directions. *Bismarck* sank early the next day, her crew believing to the last that the PBY had foiled their escape.

The battle against the U-Boats didn't need such elaborate deceptions, but there were still limits on what the British could do without revealing their secret. They settled for diverting convoys away from concentrations of U-Boats, and forming roving escort groups to reinforce convoys that were seriously threatened. It was enough. Losses remained painful, and they fluctuated for the rest of that year, but the worst seemed to be over.

CHAPTER 10: DRUMBEAT OF DISASTER

On December 7, 1941, the Imperial Japanese Navy attacked the US military base at Pearl Harbor and abruptly dragged the USA into the war. Hitler declared war the same day, committing the US Navy to an active role in the Battle of the Atlantic. That was a painful experience. Many US ships had been working closely with the British and Canadians for months, helping to escort convoys in the western Atlantic, and their crews had a good understanding of the U-Boat threat. Sadly, the same didn't apply to all their commanders. The officer in charge of home-based US Navy ships, Admiral Ernest King, didn't like the British and refused to take their advice. Instead of being formed into escorted convoys, US coastal shipping was left to carry on as before. King also didn't order a blackout along the east coast, because he didn't want to harm tourism and other businesses, so towns and highways remained brightly lit. The ships themselves doused every light on board but that was no help. From out at sea, where the gray wolves of the *U-Boot-Waffe* were gathering, their black silhouettes were clearly visible against the glowing shoreline. The submarine commanders couldn't believe their eyes.

Realizing what an easy target was being presented, Admiral Dönitz threw every long-range U-Boat he had at the east coast. Officially known as Operation Drumbeat, the men on the boats called it the Second Happy Time.

It was a massacre. Every night the U-Boats slipped quietly in towards the US coast, conning towers barely breaking the surface, and lay a couple of miles offshore, waiting. Sooner or later, the dark outline of a ship would appear. If it was a tanker, a warship or a big freighter the U-Boat would launch a torpedo; small coasters were simply blasted with the deck gun. The U-Boats only pulled off the coast to rearm from the huge *Milchkuh* supply submarines that had followed them across the Atlantic. Out in the open ocean the ships heading for Britain were gathered into tight, escorted convoys and Turing's Hut 8 routed them around the worst of the submarine activity. In Admiral King's office, the daily submarine location reports from England were ignored, requests to build escort ships were refused, and any mention of the convoy system was angrily shouted down. The slaughter continued. With all the long-range Type IX boats already in US waters, Dönitz pulled many of the standard Type VII submarines back from the convoy battle, had them crammed with extra fuel and rations and sent them to the east coast as well. Losses in

December 1941 had been 120,070 tons. In January 1942 that jumped to 327,357. By February more boats had arrived and the toll was 476,451 tons. The USA was supplying Britain with old destroyers under the Lend-Lease scheme, but in frustration at the growing carnage on the coast the Royal Navy turned over brand-new escort frigates built in Canada to the US Navy. Lack of ships wasn't the problem, though. In mid-January, when *U-123* ran amok within sight of Long Island and sank seven ships in a week, there were thirteen US Navy destroyers tied up in New York Harbor doing nothing. King didn't order them to sea. In fact, King did nothing about the U-Boats at all, even when over half a million tons of shipping was wiped out in March. His inaction couldn't have come at a worse time; unknown to him – because he hadn't been listening – disaster had struck on February 1.

German radio traffic was split into a large number of different nets, each using its own key settings, which were given names by Bletchley. At first they named them after colors; when they ran out of colors they switched to plants and animals. The net for routine German naval traffic was called *Dolphin*, but messages to and from the U-Boats went out on a separate net. The Germans had their own names for the keys and they called this one *Triton*, after the messenger god of the seas. Bletchley's name was more descriptive; the U-Boat net was called *Shark*.

Shark, like *Dolphin* and a few other naval nets, used the M3 and Hut 8 could break it at least two or three days a week. Throughout January 1942 they fed a steady stream of information to the Submarine Tracking Room in

London, from where it was fed to the convoys and –
with increasing desperation – to the deaf ears of Admiral King. Up to midnight, Berlin time, on January 31 all
was well. Then, at Dönitz's headquarters in St Nazaire
and on every U-Boat at sea, the remains of the old key
sheets were burned. New sheets were taken out from the
locked cabinet under the captain's bunk and laid on the
radio shack desk beside the Enigma machine. On each
boat a junior officer or NCO stripped the Enigma of its
cables and rotors, wiped its complex innards with an oily
rag then began to set it up for the new day's key. Plugs
snapped crisply into the stecker board and rotors
clunked into place in the guts of the machine. Each
component was carefully checked against the key setting
to make sure it was correct. Finally the operators closed
the covers, powered up the machines and turned the rotors to the message key for the day's first transmission.
Four rotors.

The German high command didn't believe Enigma could
be broken, but Admiral Dönitz wasn't quite so sure.
Sometime in late 1941 he had asked the naval cryptol-
graphy department to look at ways of increasing the security of the machines carried by his beloved U-Boats.
They came up with a simple, ingenious solution. Starting with the reflector from an M3, they designed a new
"thin" reflector that was only half as wide. Two different
versions of it were produced, each with completely new
wiring. Then they produced two "thin" rotors. These
weren't interchangeable with the existing rotors I-VIII,
so they were named Beta and Gamma to make them easily distinguishable. Together the new reflector and rotor
were exactly as wide as the old reflector and would fit in
the same space. Then they simply cut a new window and

rotor slot in the lid of the machine, and the Enigma M4 was born.

The new fourth rotor would never be turned by the one to its right, but that didn't matter much. The naval signaling procedures put strict limits on message lengths; if any signal went over 250 characters a new message key had to be chosen, and the preferred option was one of the 22-character formats from the Short Signal Book. What mattered was that with two new rotors, each of which could be turned to 26 possible positions, there were now 52 times as many possible key settings as on the M3. The new machine could be run as an M3 – each of the new rotors could be paired with one of the thin reflectors then set to A, in which position it simulated one of the M3 reflectors – so the U-Boats could talk to surface ships; that's how they'd been using January's keys. Now, however, all *Shark* traffic was 52 times as secure as *Dolphin*. Once again Bletchley was blacked out.

The bombes could be modified to work on M4 messages, but their run time turned out to be between fifty and a hundred times longer than for M3 intercepts. That meant that by the time a message was read it would already be out of date; they needed to read *Shark* traffic quickly enough to protect the convoys, and a week was far too long. Turing realized that what was needed was a much faster bombe, but he couldn't see how one could be produced. Britain's resources, both materials and manpower, were running low after three years of war. He decided to investigate having one built in the USA, but meanwhile a stopgap solution was needed. Finally he found one. It lay in *U-110*'s Short Signal Book.

Information sent by U-Boats was often of interest to German naval airbases and surface ships too, but they didn't have M4 machines. Sometimes the U-Boats would rig their machines as M3s and send the information directly in *Dolphin*, but more often they sent it to the St. Nazaire HQ in *Shark*. If St. Nazaire thought anyone else needed to know about it they would retransmit it – in *Dolphin*. Turing moved into the Crib Room and started looking at the exact times on the stacks of message forms that arrived every day. If a message came out of St. Nazaire shortly after a signal was sent from a U-Boat, he guessed that the HQ might be repeating the submarine's message. The signal from St. Nazaire would be broken as top priority and Hut 8 would then encode it using the Short Signal Book. If they'd guessed right their message would match the original signal from the U-Boat – it would be a perfect crib. Even with the increased complexity of the M4, they slowly started to break some messages again. It wasn't enough, though.

In April, the US Navy ordered coastal shipping to sail in convoy if possible, and to only move in daylight; there was still no coastal blackout because of opposition from business owners. That month *U-85* was sunk by USS *Roper*, the first loss to the Germans in the coastal campaign. In May a full convoy system was brought in and a blackout finally enforced. Ten Royal Navy corvettes and 24 armed trawlers were transferred to the east coast of the USA, the Royal Canadian Navy set up patrols off Boston, and an RAF anti-submarine squadron moved to Rhode Island to protect New York Harbor. The British and Canadians, already veterans of more than two years of anti-submarine warfare, took over patrolling in the Caribbean.[xix] Losses along the coast fell dramatically.

Unfortunately, total shipping losses through the rest of 1942 included the highest of the war – 700,235 tons in June, 729,160 in November. With *Shark* still mostly unreadable, the U-Boats simply had too much freedom to operate as they wanted. The improved security on the coast had brought losses down, but it had brought them down to the same dismally high level as they were further out at sea. Something had to be done.

The USA had been interested in Bletchley Park even before Pearl Harbor. In January 1941, two officers from the US Army and two more from the US Navy had visited the station for ten days. They'd brought a replica of the Japanese "Purple" cypher machine, and taken away a stack of documents and a paper Enigma simulator (as well as a naval radio direction-finding unit like the ones the British were using along their coasts). Admiral King might not want to hear about Station X but the US military's cryptological services certainly did; the facility was unlike anything they had themselves. Now, in July 1942, they were suddenly offered full access in exchange for help in building faster bombes. Turing passed over the plans for his bombe design to the US Navy, and by September, $2 million in funding had been authorized to research an improved design. On October 2, a US-UK agreement was signed between Bletchley and the US Navy codebreaking office, OP-20-G. Now all they had to do was wait, probably several months, for the improved bombe to be designed and put into production. Leaders on both sides of the Atlantic wondered how many ships would be left by then.

But suddenly, in late October, there was another pinch. Just after dawn on October 30, an RAF Sunderland patrol plane spotted *U-559* off the Egyptian coast. The Sunderland called in five destroyers; the first one to arrive, HMS *Hero*, forced the submarine to dive in mid-morning and for the next 16 hours the ships pounded the boat with depth-charges. Damage finally brought her up after dark. Unluckily for her she surfaced close to HMS Petard, which immediately opened fire with her light AA guns. Already close to panic the U-Boat men began abandoning ship, and in their rush, they forgot to set the demolition charges or open the seacocks. Immediately, three men from Petard's crew – one of them a NAAFI[4] canteen assistant – jumped into the sea and swam to the battered submarine. Lieutenant Anthony Fasson and Able Seaman Colin Grazier scrambled down into the hull and retrieved the key settings for October and November, plus the Short Weather Code Book. They handed these out to NAAFI assistant Tommy Brown then went back to recover the M4 itself. Sadly they were still trying to get the machine out when the damaged U-Boat suddenly sank, taking them both down with her. Brown, who'd been on the conning tower, found himself in the water with the documents. Amazingly, he managed to keep them dry. One splash and they would have been useless – they were printed in red water-soluble ink on pink paper. However he kept them safe until a boat recovered him, and by early November they were in Turing's hands.

The Short Weather Code was similar to the Short Signal system – it let U-Boats send regular weather reports in a standard, secure format. Short signals were only sent when there was something worth mentioning, though.

---

[4] The British equivalent of AAFES.

The boats out in the Atlantic each sent weather reports several times a day in *Shark*. Then the reported weather was retransmitted from St. Nazaire - in *Dolphin*, and sometimes even in clear. With the Short Weather Code to work from, Bletchley could now construct reliable cribs for *Shark* traffic. Even without a fast four-rotor bombe they had a way back in to the U-Boat messages. December's shipping losses were less than half of November's and after a blip in March and April 1943 they never went above 300,000 tons a month again. By late 1943, any more than 100,000 tons was considered a bad month.

In December 1942, Bletchley was asked to send a liaison officer to the USA. Turing was chosen because of his outstanding knowledge of the bombe – he had designed it, after all. Now he was taken to the National Cash Register Corporation plant in Dayton. Ohio and shown the prototype US Navy bomb. This had 64 drums, simulating sixteen M4 machines, and a built-in printer to print out the details of every stop. Best of all, the fastest drums turned at 1,750rpm – 35 times faster than the first British bombe. OP-20-G told him they planned to build 336, one for each possible rotor order, to achieve the fastest possible breaks. Turing explained how Banburismus could be used to reduce that number and the order was cut to 96.[xx] In the end, 121 US Navy bombes were built and many of them were shipped to Britain. To reduce the possible damage from air raids, most of the British bombes had been moved out of Bletchley to remote sites linked by secure telegraph lines. Now, thanks to a fast, encrypted transatlantic cable, the Park could use bombes located in the USA as easily as those in England. The first of the US bombes began testing on

May 3, 1943. By late June, two were running and had already broken their first *Kriegsmarine* keys. From then until the end of the war, a constant stream of intercepts, cribs, recovered keys and deciphered messages flowed back and forth between Bletchley and OP-20-G.

Turing, still in the USA, next moved on to Bell Labs where a team was working on another idea he had proposed: a voice scrambler for telephone lines. This seems to have sparked his interest; when he returned to the UK he didn't return to his job in Hut 8 but acted as a floating cryptanalyst for awhile, then moved out of the Park entirely. He was always impatient with routine, and now that *Shark* had been conclusively broken he found it boring. It was time for a new challenge and he found it at the Radio Security Service. Now known as Her Majesty's Government Communications Centre, this agency's job is to provide secure communications for the British government. Turing had now come full circle; from breaking enemy code systems he had moved to creating friendly ones. For the rest of the war he worked on scrambler systems, both at RSS and in the USA at Bell Labs. In 1943 the US Army bought SIGSALY, the system he'd helped design on his first visit to Bell in 1942. This was a very large scrambler unit – it weighed over 50 tons – used for the highest level of communications. A dozen were built in all. The first was installed in the Pentagon with an extension to The White House; the second went into the basement of Selfridge's department store in London, where General Eisenhower had his HQ; this one was also used by Winston Churchill.

Turing also helped develop a more compact device called Delilah; it was small and light enough to be carried in a large briefcase. Delilah was completed when the war was already winding down and it was never adopted, but it was an educational experience. The other major contributor to the project was Donald Bayley, an electronics expert, and he taught Turing a lot about electronics. This was to be very important later.

Ironically, Turing left Bletchley Park as another project he had initiated started to produce results. Much of the highest level German traffic wasn't encyphered on Enigma at all; it used secure teleprinter links secured with the extremely complex 12-rotor Lorenz SZ machine. This operated in a key named *Tunny*, and in July 1942, Turing had developed a technique for working out the rotor settings that was named "Turingey" or *Turingismus*. Banburismus was also used against the Lorenz machine, but Turing's priority at the time was *Shark*. To assist the *Tunny* team he introduced them to Tommy Flowers, an electrical engineer at the Post Office Research Station. He had already introduced Flowers to Max Newman, a mathematician and cryptanalyst, and after he returned to Hut 8 and the nightmare of the U-Boat cyphers the Tunny team started developing their own equivalent of the bombe. The first attempt was the Heath Robinson,[5] a bizarre skeletal contraption that used punched tape and light sensors to guess key settings. It worked, but it was slow and unreliable. Flowers could see potential in it, though. Most of the problems occurred in the electro-mechanical parts of the device; its limited electronics worked much better. In his own time he started work on

---

[5] William Heath Robinson was a British cartoonist. In 1902 he began drawing sketches of absurdly complex machines, similar to the later Rube Goldberg drawings.

an improved version that eliminated many of the moving parts and expanded the electronics. Heath Robinson contained about a dozen valves. Flowers's new device had 1,600 and worked much faster. Nicknamed Colossus for its immense size and complexity, the prototype was successfully tested at the PO Research Station on December 8, 1943, then dismantled and delivered to Bletchley Park. It and the nine improved 2,400-valve models that followed were used for the rest of the war to break *Tunny* traffic - but they were capable of a lot more. The fully electronic design meant that if the right instructions were loaded into it through its tape reader it could perform any computing task; it was the first fully programmable electronic computer. It was a Turing Machine.

CHAPTER 11: PEACETIME

When the Second World War ended, millions of servicemen and war workers began to demobilize and return home. Most of them were bursting with stories about what they'd done, and for decades to come these would be repeated weekly over a pint of beer at the local Royal British Legion Club. The armed forces shrank back toward their peacetime strength and the hostilities-only soldiers, sailors and airmen started rebuilding their interrupted lives.

GC&CS also started to shed staff. On May 8, 1945, the last Enigma machine had fallen silent; the Japanese Section's work was done on September 2. The Wrens who had operated the bombes were posted to other units, many of the civilian workers were paid off and security teams ruthlessly weeded the Park's vast archives. Most of the machines and documents were destroyed. In 1946

GC&CS was renamed Government Communications Headquarters (GCHQ) and moved to a new site at Eastcote. In 1951 it moved again, to Cheltenham, where it remains today in a vast donut-shaped building. The Park was stripped bare and sold off, and its staff scattered.

None of them talked.

Bound by the Official Secrets Act and, more importantly, a fierce loyalty to their team and what it had done, the codebreakers stayed silent until 1974; some of the survivors still won't talk. There were good reasons for that. Almost as soon as the guns stopped in Europe, tension began to rise between the western Allies and Stalin's USSR. Churchill, and his successor Attlee, knew that the ability to break Soviet codes might be vital. They didn't want the notoriously paranoid Stalin to know their capabilities.

There was also the rest of the world to think about. By the mid-1940s it was obvious that most of Britain's extensive colonies would soon be independent, but the mother country wanted to keep a maternal eye on them. There was a simple solution. The British had captured their first Enigma machine in May 1941, U-110's M3. By the end of the war, they had over a dozen of them. Then came the surrender. The British occupation zone took in almost a quarter of Germany and in it were hundreds of air bases, army headquarters and major railway stations (which also had Enigmas). Much of the German fleet, including dozens of U-Boats, was in British hands. Suddenly they had thousands of Enigma machines. Many of them were damaged; many more were older or unusual models. In among them were hundreds of Enigma-I and

M3 models, though. These were refurbished and, through the late 1940s and 1950s, handed over to the newly independent nations of the British Common-wealth. They were the best cypher machines in the world, the British assured them; absolutely unbreakable. At Cheltenham, a few surviving bombes continued to spin.

The secrecy that shrouded Bletchley Park helped pre-serve an invaluable intelligence tool, but it made it diffi-cult to reward the Park's achievements. Winston Churchill said that Turing made the single biggest con-tribution to the Allied victory,[xxi] and that deserved recognition, but it had to be discreet. In 1945, he was quietly awarded the Order of the British Empire by the King. He was also offered a job at the National Physics Laboratory, and the opportunity to build on what Tom-my Flowers had accomplished with Colossus.

The USA had started building a large electronic comput-er, ENIAC, in 1943. By 1945 it was nearing completion, and the British didn't want to be left behind. The NPL's task was to design and build its own computer, to be known as the Automatic Computing Engine. Turing's pre-War work on computable numbers made him well qualified for a post there; what he'd done at Bletchley Park, Bell Labs and RSS clinched the deal. In January 1946 he presented a paper to the NPL Executive Com-mittee describing the design of a stored-program com-puter. The problem was that his colleagues didn't – couldn't – know about Colossus and they didn't believe Turing's design would work. He knew it would, but he couldn't tell them how. He also wanted to bring in Tommy Flowers to handle the actual engineering, but again, security ruled that out. Unconvinced by his assurances, the NPL decided to build a smaller trial machine first, the Pilot Model ACE.

The US computer, ENIAC, started running in February 1946, less than a month after Turing's presentation. A more advanced successor, EDVAC, was already under construction. That put the pressure on the NPL, who were well aware that such a computer would be essential for designing hydrogen bombs; the USA, backpedalling on the cooperation agreement that had established the Manhattan Project, was trying to shut Britain out of any further nuclear weapons development. The UK wasn't going to accept that, so a working computer was urgently required.

The Pilot ACE powered up on May 10, 1950, and vindicated all of Turing's predictions. Unlike EDVAC it used subroutines – preset tasks that could be used for a variety of purposes - making it much faster to create new programs. It also had a structured programming language, Abbreviated Computer Instructions, providing a standardized way to write code for it; EDVAC required custom code for every task. The Pilot ACE could store 384 instructions in its memory, each of 32 bits, and ran at a clock speed of 1Mhz. It was the fastest computer in the world.

It didn't hold that status for long. EDVAC switched on in 1951, and while it wasn't as easily programmable as the Pilot ACE, and was plagued with reliability problems and unexplained crashes, it had double the memory and a slightly higher raw speed. By 1958, it had been upgraded significantly. By that time, NPL had gone on to build

MOSAIC, an improved version of the full ACE design. It was activated in 1952 or early 1953; its career is still shrouded in secrecy, so it's likely that it did eventually help design Britain's first hydrogen bomb. The ACE design finally became the basis for the first personal computer, the Bendix G-15.

By the time the Pilot ACE was up and running, however, Turing was long gone from the NPL. Frustrated by the security restrictions that prevented him discussing much of what he knew, in late 1947 he returned to Cambridge. Over the next few months he wrote his first speculative paper on artificial intelligence, discussing the possibility that a computer could function like a human brain. It wasn't published until long after his death but it laid the foundations for much of his remaining work.

In 1949, he was offered a senior research position at the University of Manchester and enthusiastically accepted it. By 1949, he was deputy director of the university's computing laboratory, which was developing an even more advanced computer. The design was past the theoretical stage by now and the engineers were busy ironing out the bugs, but Turing threw himself into writing software for it. The Manchester Mark 1 started running on June 16, 1949; its patents included 34 new features, many of which were adopted for the first IBM mainframes. It also sparked a controversy among British academics. When the machine was reported the press called it an "electronic brain." That led to a debate about whether a machine could ever truly be intelligent. Turing was sure it was possible, and he set to work on one of the most significant papers of his career. It was published in *Mind*, an influential psychology and philosophy journal, in October 1950.

Computing Machinery and Intelligence began with a blunt statement of intent: "I propose to consider the question, 'Can machines think?'"[xxii] Over the next 21 pages he calmly and logically defined "think," defined "machine," explained how a digital computer could perform the functions of a brain, then mercilessly demolished every objection to his argument. Then he went on to propose a test for artificial intelligence, one that's still the standard benchmark today.

The Turing Test is starkly simple and devastatingly effective. A machine would be intelligent, Turing said, if it could fool a human into thinking they were interacting with another human. He suggested having the human interrogator in one room, able to communicate with the computer through some kind of output device (monitors weren't in use then – most computers delivered their output on punched tape or dials). To make the experiment unbiased the interrogator shouldn't be asked to decide if they were talking to a machine; they should be asked to decide if they were talking to a man or a woman. The experiment would be run a number of times; sometimes the interrogator would be interacting with the computer and sometimes with a real human who was trying to hide their true gender. If they guessed wrongly as often when they were talking to the computer as when they were talking to a human, the machine would qualify as intelligent.

The Turing Test is now widely accepted as the hurdle a computer has to clear to be classed as intelligent. It's never been passed, despite various well-publicized claims (most recently on June 7, 2014).[xxiii] Every claimed success has used a program that analyzes the syntax and vocabulary of the human's questions and picks an appropriate response from a library. There's no actual intelligence involved, just pattern recognition. They've also used various tricks to disguise awkward replies – in the 2014 attempt the interrogator was told in advance that they were talking to a Ukrainian teenager, so any strange answers would have been written off as unfamiliarity with English. Interrogating it in Ukrainian would have produced a very different result. To legitimately pass the test the machine needs to genuinely *understand*. It hasn't happened yet, but one day it will.

CHAPTER 12: DOWNFALL

In late 1951, Turing developed a new interest, this time in biology. Genetics was in its infancy then but it was already obvious that mathematics could be applied to help understand it better. What interested Turing was how living things develop their shape, as they progress from a single cell to a complex organism. Without experimenting in a lab, working purely through equations, he developed an explanation for pattern formation in developing organisms. In 2013, scientists from the University of Pennsylvania tested his hypothesis experimentally; it was correct.[xxiv]

A year after Turing published his hypothesis Francis Crick, James Watson and Rosalind Franklin explained the structure of the DNA molecule, the chemical that controls heredity and development. DNA is often described as a code or a language. It isn't, really; it's just a molecule that can catalyze a variety of extremely complex chemical reactions, with the end product being proteins. "Code" is a good shorthand description for it though, because in some ways it behaves quite like one. Turing's unique skills could have made a massive contribution to understanding it and developing the new science of genetics. Unfortunately, he was almost out of time.

For his entire adult life, since shortly after realizing that he was gay, Turing had lived and worked in sheltered environments where his sexuality wasn't a problem. In fact, at Bletchley he'd briefly been engaged to a female Hut 8 cryptanalyst, Joan Clarke. He proposed to her in the spring of 1941; when he told her a few days later that he had "homosexual tendencies" she was undismayed, and the relationship continued. They spent days off and vacations together and he bought her a ring, although to keep the engagement secret she didn't wear it at work. He even told her he wanted to have children.[xxv] However, Turing broke off the engagement later that year, feeling that his sexuality would doom the marriage to failure.

Now he was working in the outside world. Manchester University was very different from the cloistered atmosphere of Cambridge or the eccentric environment of Bletchley Park. Turing wasn't cocooned in the closed society of King's College or Hut 8. Instead, he was living in a suburban house, eating his meals at home or in local restaurants. He'd never been above the law but now he was visible to it. He'd never had to worry much about crime, either, beyond the risk of some unfortunate thief who might want to make off with his temperamental bike. Manchester was different.

In December 1951, not long after he began his work on biology, Turing was walking through central Manchester when he met a young man just outside the movie theater on Oxford Road. They struck up a conversation and Turing invited him for lunch. Later he asked the young man, Arnold Murray, to come to his house that weekend. Murray didn't show up, but in January 1952, they bumped into each other again and soon began a relationship.

Unfortunately Turing, perhaps made naïve by the sheltered life he'd led, had chosen badly. Murray stole £10 (almost $1,150 in 2014 dollars) from Turing's wallet, although when Turing confronted him about it Murray managed to half-convince him he wasn't guilty. Nevertheless, when the house was burgled on January 23 he suspected Murray of being involved.[xxvi]

Now Turing moved onto thin ice. He reported the burglary to the police. That was reasonable enough, and clear-up rates were far higher then than they are today, but it brought the scrutiny of the law dangerously close to home and his private life couldn't stand much scrutiny. The police visited his house and fingerprinted it, then started checking through their records. Meanwhile Turing wrote to Murray, telling him that their relationship was over and bringing up the missing money. In response, Murray turned up at his door, angrily denying any knowledge of the cash. In the end they had a reconciliation. Afterward, Murray said that he suspected an acquaintance of his, an unemployed man named Harry, of having broken into the house. Then Turing made a fatal mistake.

Still suspecting Murray of the burglary, he wrapped up a glass the young man had handled and took it to the police along with a story explaining how he came to have it. It was a risk, and an unnecessary one – they'd already identified Harry as the burglar from fingerprints found in the house. Turing's story raised new suspicions though, and they began questioning him. The interrogation was mild at first, then more pointed, and the shy, awkward academic wasn't equipped to handle it. Finally confronted with a straight accusation of homosexuality, he told the truth in an attempt to stop the questions. Immediately, he was arrested for "Gross Indecency".

The United Kingdom's Criminal Law Amendment Act of 1885 had a vague paragraph, Section 11, calling for up to two years' imprisonment for any man found guilty of gross indecency with another man, whether in public or private. The law didn't spell out what the offence actually was but everyone knew it meant gay sex.[6] In 1895, Section 11 had been used to send Oscar Wilde to his famous confinement in Reading Gaol. Now it was turned against Alan Turing.

Turing was tried on March 31, and his defense should have been a strong one. He was called a "national asset" for his work on computing, and his OBE was mentioned along with hints of vital war work that couldn't be re-

---

[6] Oddly only male homosexuality was covered; Queen Victoria, who as sovereign had to approve all laws, refused to allow any mention of lesbians.

vealed. Guy Burgess and Donald Maclean had recently been unmasked as Soviet spies, though, and there was little tolerance for a man seen as just one more Cambridge-educated "poofter" with a head full of secrets he should never have been trusted with. In strict legal terms, the verdict was inevitable anyway; he'd admitted his "offence" to the detectives investigating the burglary. In an attempt to ease the probable sentence, he pleaded guilty to the charge.

Perhaps that strategy worked. He could have been sentenced to two years' jail with no alternative. Instead he was given an option; he could avoid prison if he agreed to go on probation and undergo hormone treatment. He accepted.

The hormone treatment involved injections of synthetic estrogen, intended to reduce the libido. "It is supposed to reduce sexual urge while it goes on, but one is supposed to return to normal when it is over. I hope they're right," he wrote to a friend two weeks after the trial.[xxvii] But his life could never return to normal.

Homosexuality was a crime under British law, but in the secret world Turing had moved in it was viewed even more seriously. Homosexuals could be blackmailed, and if they possessed valuable secrets, that made them easy targets for foreign spies. It never seems to have occurred to anyone that the only reason gay men could be blackmailed was that they faced criminal charges if exposed. Instead, the response was to remove them from any position dealing with sensitive information. Members of the armed forces could be administratively discharged as late as 2000, 32 years after homosexuality was decrimi-

nalized; there was certainly no possibility of passing security vetting. Turing had held top-level security clear-
ances since 1938 but now they were revoked. After being
at the heart of the intelligence services for six years,
then working on the nation's most advanced technology
projects, that door was slammed in his face forever.

For the next two years, Turing continued with his biology research but his heart didn't seem to be in it any
more. He also suffered horrific side-effects from the
"therapy," which turned out to amount to chemical cas-
tration. He grew breasts from the estrogen injections
and began to fall into bouts of deep depression. It quickly grew so bad he had to start seeing a therapist, a rare
and grave step in the early 1950s. Finally, it seems, he'd
had enough.

On June 7, 1954 Turing's cleaner, worried at the silence
in the house, pushed open the door of his bedroom. She
found him in bed, lifeless. An autopsy was performed
and the cause of death was found to be cyanide poison-
ing. But the cryptographic genius had left one last enigma behind, one that only he had the solution to. How
was he poisoned?

Turing had been carrying out experiments involving
electroplating teaspoons with gold; he'd been using a
solution of gold dissolved in potassium cyanide, legally
bought from a chemical supplier, and a home-built appa-
ratus set up in his spare room. There's been speculation
that the device started to release hydrogen cyanide gas
and Turing, on the point of being overcome, staggered
through to his bedroom before collapsing.[xxviii] However,
there was also an apple with a single, almost symbolic

bite taken out of it, sitting on the bedside table. Most people believe that the apple had been dipped in, or injected with, cyanide. That seems the most likely explanation for two reasons. Hydrogen cyanide is an extremely fast-acting blood agent, and if Turing had accidentally poisoned himself with it there's little chance he'd have made it out of the spare room. Secondly, Turing's favorite fairy tale was *Snow White.* In the 1937 Disney version he loved the scene where the Wicked Queen dips an apple in poison.[xxix]

Alan Mathison Turing was cremated on June 12, 1954. Unlike the Enigma machine he took his final secret to the grave.

CHAPTER 13: REHABILITATION

Society has changed beyond recognition in the sixty years since Alan Turing died. The relationship that ended his career - and ultimately his life - wouldn't even attract comment in Britain today. It certainly wouldn't have affected his security clearance. Given what he'd done for his country Turing was treated appallingly, and it took a long time for the government to officially recognize that. Eventually it happened, though. In 2009 an online petition to issue a belated apology attracted over 30,000 signatures, including many from prominent scientists.[xxx] It was heard. On September 10 that year Prime Minister Gordon Brown described Turing's treatment as "horrifying" and "utterly unfair" and announced, on behalf of the nation, "We're sorry. You deserved so much better." Turing's reputation, almost forgotten for so many years, had started to revive since *TIME* Magazine named him as one of the hundred most important people of the 20th century, and now the momentum to formally clear his name was becoming unstoppable. Another petition in 2011 asked for him to be given a formal pardon and collected 37,000 names. It was declined, but his supporters didn't give up; a group of peers, including former Hut 8 linguist Lady Trumpington, introduced a bill in the House of Lords demanding action. Before it could make it all the way through Parliament, Queen Elizabeth II issued a royal pardon – only the fourth since the end of the war.

The decision to pardon Turing wasn't uncontroversial. There's no doubt he was guilty of an offence under the law of his time, even if the law is now seen as unjust. Most of the controversy played out online, though, in a striking example of just how influential he had been. The World Wide Web was invented by Tim Berners-Lee, on the foundation laid by DARPA, but the modern computers it runs on can be traced back to Turing's papers of 1936 and 1946. The connected world we live in today was built on his work.

And so was the freedom we enjoy. That freedom isn't unlimited, of course, and the constraints placed on it are rightly the subject of many more fierce debates, but the world is a lot freer than it would have been if Admiral Dönitz's U-Boats had starved Britain into submission and left Hitler the master of Europe. It's unlikely that the USA would have fallen to either Germany or Japan, but faced with militarized fascist empires across the oceans to both east and west, could it have survived as the open democracy it is today - or would it have had to militarize in turn to meet the constant threat?

Turing

Thanks to Alan Turing we never had to find out.

---

[i] LondonTown.com, *London's Autumn Hotels*

http://www.londontown.com/London/Autumn_Hotels_2006?sea
rchCriteria=WARRINGTON CRESCENT#featureContent3547HEAD

[ii] The Alan Turing Internet Scrapbook, *Alan Turing's Early Life, 1912-1928*
  http://www.turing.org.uk/scrapbook/early.html

[iii] System Toolbox, *Alan Turing – Towards a Digital Mind: Part 1*
  http://www.systemtoolbox.com/article.php?history_id=3

[iv] Kent and Sussex Courier, December 21, 2012, *Schoolboy showed signs of brilliance to follow*
  http://www.courier.co.uk/Schoolboy-showed-signs-brilliance-follow/story-17647286-detail/story.html

[v] Hodges, A. (1983), *Alan Turing: The Enigma*
  http://www.turing.org.uk/book/extracts/ext1-33.html

[vi] The Alan Turing Internet Scrapbook, *The Inspiration of Life and Death, 1928-1932*
  http://www.turing.org.uk/scrapbook/spirit.html

[vii] Polari Magazine, Jun 23, 2013, *How A Gay Love Story Led To The Invention Of The Computer*
  http://www.polarimagazine.com/features/gay-love-story-led-invention-computer/

[viii] Princeton University (1985), *Interview with Alonzo Church*

http://www.princeton.edu/~mudd/finding_aids/mathoral/pmc05.htm

[ix] McKay, S. (2010), *The Secret Life of Bletchley Park*

[x] Cryptologia, July 2005; Sullivan, G. & Weierud, F., *Breaking German Army Cyphers*
  http://www.tandf.co.uk/journals/pdf/papers/ucry_06.pdf

[xi] Cypher Machines & Cryptology, *Kurzsignalen on German U-boats*
  http://users.telenet.be/d.rijmenants/pics/codebook3.jpg

[xii] McKay, S. (2010), *The Secret Life of Bletchley Park*

[xiii] McKay, S. (2010), *The Secret Life of Bletchley Park*

[xiv] Alexander, C.H.O'D. (1945), *Cryptographic History of Work on the German Naval Enigma*

http://www.ellsbury.com/gne/gne-020.htm

[xv] HMS *Gleaner* 1940, *Sinking of U33 and capture of Enigma machine rotors*

http://www.halcyon-class.co.uk/gleaner/gleaner_1940.htm

[xvi] Batey, Mavis (2008), *From Bletchley With Love*

[xvii] McKay, S. (2010), *The Secret Life of Bletchley Park*

[xviii] McKay, S. (2010), *The Secret Life of Bletchley Park*

[xix] Imperial War Museum, *The Battle of the Atlantic – Royal Canadian Navy 1939-1942*

http://archive.iwm.org.uk/upload/package/8/atlantic/can3942.htm

[xx] Dayton Codebreakers, *Bombe Project History, May 44*

http://daytoncodebreakers.org/depth/bombe_history2/

[xxi] The Turing Centenary, *Churchill: Turing made the single biggest contribution to the war effort*

http://theturingcentenary.wordpress.com/2011/10/19/churchill-turing-made-the-single-biggest-contribution-to-the-war-effort/

[xxii] Turing, A.M. (1950), *Computing Machinery and Intelligence*

http://orium.pw/paper/turingai.pdf

[xxiii] Science Daily, June 9, 2014, *Turing Test success marks milestone in computing history*

http://www.sciencedaily.com/releases/2014/06/140609093827.htm?+Math+News+--+ScienceDaily)

[xxiv] Tompkins et al, 2013; *Testing Turing's theory of morphogenesis in chemical cells*

http://www.pnas.org/content/early/2014/03/05/1322005111.abstract?sid=44d2b445-66f5-4dd1-b1c0-d6c25e88accb

[xxv] University of St Andrews, *Joan Elizabeth Lowther Clarke Murray*

http://www-history.mcs.st-and.ac.uk/Biographies/Clarke_Joan.html

[xxvi] Polari Magazine, June 12, 2012, *Turing Centenary: The Trial of Alan Turing for Homosexual Conduct*

http://www.polarimagazine.com/features/turing-centenary-trial-alan-turing-homosexual-conduct/

[xxvii] Polari Magazine, June 12, 2012, *Turing Centenary: The Trial of Alan Turing for Homosexual Conduct*

http://www.polarimagazine.com/features/turing-centenary-trial-alan-turing-homosexual-conduct/

[xxviii] BBC News. June 26, 2012, *Alan Turing: Inquest's suicide verdict 'not supportable'*

http://www.bbc.com/news/science-environment-18561092

[xxix] Hodges, A. (1983), *Alan Turing: The Enigma*

[xxx] The Guardian, September 11, 2009, *PM's apology to codebreaker Alan Turing: we were inhumane*

http://www.theguardian.com/world/2009/sep/11/pm-apology-to-alan-turing

CPSIA information can be obtained
at www.ICGtesting.com
Printed in the USA
LVOW08s2248050217
523296LV00003B/264/P